Life-Changing Synchronicities

"This book is a true odyssey, filled with mesmerizing synchronicities and moments of divine alignment that ignite the reader's own sense of wonder. With each page, Bernie takes us into the heart of the magical coincidences that have shaped his life, weaving a tapestry of profound experiences and spiritual awakenings. Bernie's courageous storytelling opens a gateway to understanding how synchronicity can be a guiding force that helps us discover our full potential and tap into a life of deeper meaning. Read this book and allow it to awaken in you a new appreciation for the mysteries that shape our lives. It's a journey well worth taking."

MAUREEN J. ST. GERMAIN, AUTHOR OF
LIVING YOUR BEST 5D LIFE AND *WAKING UP IN 5D*

"This is a rare personal invitation to view behind the scenes into the deep well of inspiration that has guided and shaped Beitman's life. Filled with wise anecdotes, this charming book entertains as much as it educates—a truly delightful read."

JOSEPH CAMBRAY, PH.D., PAST PRESIDENT OF
PACIFICA GRADUATE INSTITUTE AND AUTHOR OF *SYNCHRONICITY*

"Scientism would like us to believe that no meaningful connections exist among events because there is no point to the universe. However, quantum physics is very clear about the existence of entanglement, proving that all events are interconnected in ways beyond what human instruments can detect. Throughout Beitman's book hovers the sense that synchronistic events exist because there is order, purpose, and meaning in the universe. I also believe from experience that synchronicities are the way in which the universe communicates to us in ways that are relevant to our life's journey, thus enlightening and comforting us."

FEDERICO FAGGIN, PHYSICIST, INVENTOR OF
THE MICROPROCESSOR, AND AUTHOR OF *IRREDUCIBLE*

"I love Bernie Beitman's new autobiographical take on meaningful coincidences! He writes vividly and engagingly about his synchronistically patterned life at various phases, including his athletic prowess and hippie psychedelic experiences as well as his professional career. Readers can draw their own lessons and insights from his 'doctor's notes' and formulation of principles to better understand patterns in their own lives. Compulsive reading!"

DAVID LORIMER, PROGRAM DIRECTOR OF THE
SCIENTIFIC & MEDICAL NETWORK AND
AUTHOR OF *A QUEST FOR WISDOM*

"Synchronicities are natural and revelatory phenomena of the emergent understanding of a living universe that meaningfully exists and purposefully evolves as a unified entity. *Life-Changing Synchronicities* is itself a synchronicity as a way-shower, helping guide us to more consciously align both with our own life path and with the evolutionary impulse of our entire universe."

JUDE CURRIVAN, PH.D., AUTHOR OF
THE STORY OF GAIA AND *THE COSMIC HOLOGRAM*

"Beitman masterfully assembled a wonderful collection of autobiographical accounts of how personal meaningful coincidences and synchronicities have woven an ongoing story throughout his life. As a timeless resource, the reader can use this book as a personal guide to a heightened awareness of interconnected synchronicity experiences on their own ongoing life journey."

THOMAS E. MYERS, PH.D., BEHAVIORAL AND
ORGANIZATIONAL DEVELOPMENT ADVISOR

"*Life-Changing Synchronicities* offers us delightful stories of synchronicity from the life of a psychiatrist who has studied this phenomenon throughout his career. Beitman invites readers to pay close attention to the deep and magical interconnections we experience with other people, animals, and even nature, and to re-enchant our lives in the process."

MARJORIE WOOLLACOTT, PH.D.,
COEDITOR OF *THE PLAYFUL UNIVERSE*

Life-Changing Synchronicities

A Doctor's Journey of Coincidence and Serendipity

A Sacred Planet Book

Bernard Beitman, M.D.

Park Street Press
Rochester, Vermont

Park Street Press
One Park Street
Rochester, Vermont 05767
www.ParkStPress.com

Park Street Press is a division of Inner Traditions International

Sacred Planet Books are curated by Richard Grossinger, Inner Traditions editorial board member and cofounder and former publisher of North Atlantic Books. The Sacred Planet collection, published under the umbrella of the Inner Traditions family of imprints, includes works on the themes of consciousness, cosmology, alternative medicine, dreams, climate, permaculture, alchemy, shamanic studies, oracles, astrology, crystals, hyperobjects, locutions, and subtle bodies.

Cataloging-in-Publication Data for this title is available from the Library of Congress

ISBN 979-8-88850-184-9 (print)
ISBN 979-8-88850-185-6 (ebook)

Printed and bound in the United States by Lake Book Manufacturing, LLC

10 9 8 7 6 5 4 3 2 1

Text design by Virginia Scott Bowman and layout by Debbie Glogover
This book was typeset in Garamond Premier Pro with Begum, Belda, Futura Std, Gill Sans MT Pro, and Myriad Pro used as display typefaces

To send correspondence to the author of this book, mail a first-class letter to the author c/o Inner Traditions • Bear & Company, One Park Street, Rochester, VT 05767, and we will forward the communication, or contact the author directly at **coincider.com**.

To
Carl Jung

Contents

PART 2

Serial Coincidences

Foreword

Roderick Main

IN MAINSTREAM MODERN CULTURES, coincidences are not generally accorded much importance. They may be experienced as personally striking, even deeply meaningful, but ultimately, it is assumed, they are due either to mere chance or to ordinary causes that just happen not yet to have been uncovered in that specific case. There is no need to think about them in any other way.

In many premodern cultures, by contrast, what we would call coincidences enjoyed a much greater significance and were often viewed as affording deep insight into reality. Witness the worldwide occurrence of divination practices, which fundamentally depend on interpreting coincidental events. Most such practices presuppose a radical interconnectedness or unity of reality in which what happens in the mind or at the human level and what happens in the world or at a cosmic level match each other and express a deeper order of meaning. In such a view, coincidences, rightly interpreted, can speak to us from that deeper order.

With the rise of science from the seventeenth century and the rapid, successful application of causal thinking, the view that events could be connected acausally through meaning was marginalized and increasingly treated as superstition or intellectual weakness. However, the scientific mode of thinking that became dominant has been perceived by many to entrain problems of its own. One influential articulation of these problems is Max Weber's notion that the world has become disenchanted: in effect, stripped of genuine mystery, lacking in inherent meaning, and unrelated to any spiritual or divine reality.[1] Weber himself thought this condition was an unavoidable consequence of modernity and needed to be accepted alongside all the undeniable benefits of science and technology. Others, however, have felt that the consequences of disenchantment—an overly rationalistic, bureaucratic, instrumentalist, and exploitative culture spawning the kind of social, political, and environmental crises by which we are currently beset—are too grave; it should be possible to strike a better balance between the causal thinking of science and alternative ways of attending to reality.

One figure who attempted to find such a better balance was the Swiss psychiatrist, Carl Jung. Not least, Jung's (1952/1969) seminal concept of synchronicity ("meaningful coincidence") precisely tried to recover, in modern guise, the view that events, as well as being connected through causes and effects, could also be connected acausally through meaning. Since Jung's death, there has been an ever-increasing stream of work on synchronicity by those knowledgeable about his thought, focusing on not just psychotherapy but science, religion, and a wide range of cultural and environmental issues. Most of this work, inevitably, has been bound up with other concepts of Jung's psychological model and is not always readily accessible to the general reader.

Enter another psychiatrist who has become a champion of meaningful coincidence, Dr. Bernard Beitman. As a psychiatrist, Bernie, like Jung, is concerned with the human as well as theoretical significance of coincidence. But while Bernie acknowledges the inspiration of Jung, he is not an adherent of Jungian psychology, and so his approach to coincidences is open to many more perspectives than just Jung's framework.

Over the last fifteen years or so, Bernie has been researching coincidences with astonishing zeal and has contributed as much as anyone to raising the profile of the phenomenon. He has published his ideas

---

1. See my 2022 book *Breaking the Spell of Disenchantment*.

in academic and professional articles and blogs, as well as in a series of books for a general readership, of which this is the third since 2016. He has also broadcast literally hundreds of audio and video interviews with guests who have experienced coincidences of every conceivable kind and studied them from every conceivable angle. And recently he has initiated The Coincidence Project to provide a forum for widening and deepening discussion of the topic even further. To an unprecedented degree, Bernie has opened himself up, intellectually and emotionally, to the many dimensions of the phenomenon and to the many diverse experiencers of it.

Much of Bernie's work, including his series of radio and video interviews, has been done under the banner of "Connecting with Coincidence," which was the title of his first book. The phrase is deliberately ambiguous: those who attend to coincidences find that they often realize deeper connections between themselves and others, as well as among usually unrelated areas of their experience; but they also connect increasingly to the phenomenon of coincidence itself and thus become more adept at noticing and interpreting coincidences.

But there is yet another kind of connection that Bernie's work fosters: between different levels and styles of engagement. There are many profound philosophical and cultural implications of coincidences and many subtle ways of working with them psychologically, as scholars and practitioners of Jungian psychology have especially explored, and which Bernie in due measure also explores. But not all engagement with coincidence needs to be abstruse or to be expressed in technical ways. There are many coincidences, or aspects of them, that are immediately impactful, intelligible, and transformative. Often, all that is needed is for the experiencer to attend to the event and to let the event disclose itself at the levels that are pertinent to that experiencer at that time. Bernie's approach to studying coincidences connects, in a single body of work, the whole spectrum of levels at which they can occur and be responded to. And when he describes and interprets them, his gift for clear, direct communication conveys their essence vividly. He keeps the reader in touch with the experiential core of the coincidences, and it is in doing this, above all, that he helps to foster that more balanced and holistic state of awareness—sensitive to acausal patterns of meaning as well as to causes and effects—that our time so urgently needs.

Bernie's two previous books, *Connecting with Coincidence* (2016) and *Meaningful Coincidences* (2022), are rich in examples, from which a great deal of insight and practical advice is adroitly distilled. What is distinctive about this new book is that it narrates and discusses Bernie's own experiences of coincidence across the whole span of his long life. It is an autobiography written in coincidences. It shows that Bernie had been living with and living in the phenomenon of coincidence long before he began to write about it formally.

And what a rich and colorful life it is with its episodes of sporting prowess, hippie experimentation, relational complexities, and high-level professional achievement and challenge! Perhaps the lives of all of us are similarly rich when we learn to see the intricate patterns of connection unfolding within them. With the accounts of his experiences, Bernie offers not only vivid cameos of the events themselves but also insightful commentary on how they influenced him and what wider principles, for working with coincidences or simply for living, can be elicited from them. The repeated application of this process reinforces the importance of not just experiencing coincidences but actively reflecting on them. And indeed, the need for active engagement is another theme that powerfully emerges from the book.

With its autobiographical emphasis, this book seems to me neatly to complete the project of Bernie's previous two books. One of the most important features of coincidences, at least the kind of meaningful coincidences that are also referred to as synchronicities, is that they involve a paralleling of inner psychic (subjective) states and outer physical (objective) events. In meaningful coincidences, the subjective component is as crucial as the objective component. It is therefore apt that we are shown not just what Bernie the scholar and scientist has found out from scrutiny of his objectively gathered data on coincidences, which is the primary focus of his first two books, but also what Bernie the human being and coincidence subject himself has distilled from the courageously exposed subjective data of his own experiences, which is the focus of this his third book.

This is a book that will delight, illuminate, and perhaps, above all, spur us as readers to pay greater attention to the ways in which our lives are much more deeply interconnected with one another, with the social and natural worlds more broadly, and indeed with our own pasts and futures than we normally allow ourselves to perceive. It invites us to undertake, or to further, our own adventure into this fascinating and important territory.

RODERICK MAIN is a professor in the Department of Psychosocial and Psychoanalytic Studies at the University of Essex and the author of *Breaking the Spell of Disenchantment: Mystery, Meaning, and Metaphysics in the Work of C. G. Jung* (Chiron Publications, 2022).

The Strangeness that Masquerades as Real Life

Paper is patient.
—ANNE FRANK

I'VE BEEN IN MANY PLACES in my life and times. I've encountered many coincidences and made some surprising finds. I've taken a chance on chance. Like Alice in Wonderland, I've encountered the strangeness that masquerades as real life.

I was an adventuresome and curious boy who discovered an imaginary hidden tunnel in the woods near my house. When my dog Snapper and I walked through the tunnel, a beautiful jungle was revealed, teeming with dazzling pairs and bouncy triples and occasional twirls of four. Within the repeating patterns, similarities were glowing that were strikingly familiar and simultaneously different. Opposites within opposites. I ran back through the tunnel to tell anyone who would listen. But I was mute. I could not speak. I had no words to describe what we saw. No one was there to understand except Snapper. Were they illusions or emblems of an untaught reality? Many years later I found a way to describe those dazzling shapes. These meaningful coincidences are keys to how our minds work, to our interconnectedness, and to saving ourselves from our own self-destruction.

1

Contrasts breed synchronicity and serendipity. I am an ambulating contradiction. As a scholarly, nearsighted student, I ran back kickoffs and punts during high school and college football games without glasses or contact lenses. While a psychiatric resident at an elite school, I was a part-time hippie during the ecstatic vortex of Haight-Ashbury, San Francisco, in the late 1960s. As chairman of an academic psychiatry department, I initiated a formal research project to investigate the immense promise in meaningful coincidences.

This autobiography unfurls the tapestry of meaningful coincidences across my life. They feel extraordinary to me. People often believe that their synchronicities are extraordinary. I am no exception. But to others these synchronicities may not be particularly striking. What is unique here is the sheer number of them on display over a lifetime. Some may strike you as funny. Others may seem unusual. Many will seem familiar. Taken together, they serve to illustrate common coincidence forms.

As portals to exploration and adventure, meaningful coincidences make living more interesting, surprising, and exciting. I hope you will see your own life reflected in these stories. Perhaps you will be stimulated to excavate a buried memory of a synchronicity that changed your life. You might look back over your life stories to see the recurrent patterns across them.

Writing and organizing these coincidence stories has made another more disturbing pattern in my life quite evident. To my horror, I saw the many times coincidences have led me down the wrong paths, often feeding my grandiose sense of self. By recording these stories, I am trying to dislodge from my heart, mind, and spirit the sense of my being special for having experienced these events. Instead, I am learning to be grateful for them. Many other people have similar experiences. A basic principle emerging from the study of coincidence is, *If you have some improbable coincidence, someone else has had, or will soon have, a similar experience.* Each of us is unique so we share certain uniqueness with others. In this world of polarities, each of us is both special and ordinary.

By recording these stories, I have put them behind me to seek a release from the hold some of them have had on me. I hope to get their now decaying grandiose feelings expunged, exorcised from me. This writing process enables me to more fully embrace the remainder of my days in this body and enjoy my uniqueness and my ordinariness. No one else is occupying this space at this time. No one else is occupying the space you are in at this time. We are all ordinary, unique beings in our time and our space.

You may be one of the ever-increasing number of human beings who recognizes that synchronicity offers help to our troubled species. We are increasingly disconnected from each other and from Earth's natural world. War, income disparities, isolation, loneliness, and global warming shout out: "You are not acknowledging your connections with each other!" The quiet powers of synchronicity and serendipity can aid our healing by creating experiences of connecting us to each other, to trees, to animals, and to other beings.

PERSONAL SYNCHRONICITY PATTERNS

Each of us has a personal set of patterns by which to notice and process coincidences. I have initiated a research project using artificial intelligence to seek patterns in coincidence stories and then to match people with similar patterns, something like a dating app. Hopefully, this idea will reach fruition and you will be able to find like-minded synchronicity friends to further enrich your experience of both uniqueness and similarity.

I noticed several recurring patterns in these stories.

I enjoy *being in the right place at the right time* without making a conscious decision to go there. In the chapter titled "Internal GPS," I tested out my own ability to consciously get where I wanted to be at the right time. Like flocks of birds flying to their breeding grounds or lost dogs finding their way back home, I could intuitively time my actions for really nice coincidences to happen. Others do this too. Do you? Have you activated your Human GPS?

Knocking on strangers' doors became another consequential pattern. As you will see, knocking on doors led to my taking LSD well before our society had recognized its potential. With that LSD knock came an introduction to astrology and tarot cards. Knowing these areas of study helped me adapt to the pop-up hippie culture of the late 1960s. Another knock-knock led to my securing the necessary data for the required medical school thesis. Then came a knock that led to my marrying the daughter of a past president of the American Psychoanalytic Association. And a hesitant knock on a colleague's door opened the path to becoming chair of psychiatry.

My favorite is a cartoonlike pattern that has me *swinging from vine to vine in the coincidence jungle*. I'd grab one vine attached to a certain tree, climb around on the tree, and meet other coincidence monkeys and circumstances. Sometimes I went out on a limb and needed to jump to catch another vine to another tree. From Devine to Devine, quipped a colleague. Or Coinci-Dancing, punned another. Like many potential coincidences, I had to jump to catch the next vine. Without moving, without action, many potentially great synchronicities do not happen.

With this knowledge, over time I got pretty good at imagining possibilities and helping to make them happen. This time-tested capacity soon became a guideline—*imagine something possible* and help make it happen. High emotion and strong need are often the drivers for manifesting what you imagine. Without deciding to act, the desired outcome is unlikely to happen. You violate yourself by not moving. As opposed to being ticketed and fined for driving too fast (a moving violation), you are fined by missing a potential opportunity—a "non-moving" violation.

I strive to improve what I do and expand on what I know. I love to get better at doing things. Each improvement is new learning. Each new action creates novelty.

Try looking for your own basic coincidence patterns.

Like most things on planet Earth, polarities rule. The bad comes with the good with a message that there is more to learn. What I imagined into happening sometimes became too real, injuring me psychologically or physically. Be careful, you might get what you wish for.

I learned that the less I was contained and restrained by social structures, and the more I was left to my own devices, the more coincidences arose from apparent randomness. Others have confirmed this observation.

The content of this book is filtered through my mind, expanded and limited by my experiences with the subject. Uniqueness brings limitations. My two previous books *Connecting with Coincidence* and *Meaningful Coincidences* grew out of my being objective about synchronicity and serendipity. In this book, I turn that filter inside out to show you the patterns from which those books grew. Here you will see the lived-in-the-world experiences from which I have drawn the many observations and conclusions I have made about meaningful coincidences.

Our life stories are sprinkled with coincidences. Novelists and script writers know this idea: No coincidence, no story. And that includes the story of your life.

Spiritual teachers, spiritual masters, guides, gurus, and mystics have not been central to this life journey. "If you meet the Buddha on the road, kill him!" has been closer to my guiding mantra. This imperative suggests that you should rely on yourself. I could not be a person who says, "I have a guru. I don't have to think anymore." The learning came through to me from interactions with people and the natural world, often by way of meaningful coincidences, some of which may have been orchestrated by spirit guides. You may need someone to instruct you. I suggest you have full trust in that person and/or you carefully discriminate what is being suggested. So many people now are trying to be helpful to others. They often generalize from their own experiences to everyone else. In reality, their personal experiences resonate effectively with a limited swath of humanity. Are you in that person's swath?

My adventures have led to discovering that, like fish in the sea, our minds and hearts swim in the vastness of our mental atmosphere—the psychosphere.

THE PSYCHOSPHERE

Many psycho-spiritual adventures reveal that human beings participate in a shared mind while simultaneously having a separate personal identity. Two visual metaphors for this shared mind involve the ocean, the water from which land life seems to have emerged. One describes the person as a drop hovering above the vast expanse of water that metaphorically refers to consciousness (still to be clearly defined). Gravity brings the drop back into the ocean as do various modes of self-obliteration, including death, bringing the separate self into the oneness of the ocean. Another popular visual metaphor involves islands jutting above the surface, each one separate from the other islands. Yet no person is an island alone. Draining out the water shows how the islands are mountaintops whose bases are in the ocean floor that connects them all to each other.

Water connects us all. Earth connects us all.

I propose an air metaphor. Air most closely resembles Mind. Our minds and hearts are immersed in the Earth's mental atmosphere, the psychosphere. Just as we breathe in oxygen and breathe out carbon dioxide, we "inhale" energy-information (heart-mind) from our mental atmosphere and exhale energy-information into the psychosphere.

The psychosphere includes a mental internet through which living beings can communicate with each other. The swirling energy of the psychosphere dynamically moves the contents of both the collective unconscious and the collective conscious, interpenetrating living minds and hearts.

Synchronicities illuminate many of the activities of the psychosphere. The collection of points of contact between human minds and aspects of the psychosphere provide the needed map of how it works. Knowledge of the functioning of the psychosphere can help efforts to mitigate global warming and the many injustices human beings inflict on each other by showing each of us our lived interconnectedness.

ABOUT MEANINGFUL COINCIDENCES

What is a meaningful coincidence? A coincidence is the unexpected, surprising, improbable concurrence of two or more events without apparent causal connection. It could be random or have a yet-to-be-defined explanation. It could have no meaning or could be meaningful. Coincidences may be both improbable and surprising, but these are not synonyms. Coincidences tend to be improbable events, but all improbable events aren't necessarily coincidences. For example, rolling a die six times and getting 464255 might be just as improbable as 666666, but not nearly as surprising. Similarly, coincidences are usually surprising. But events that are surprising, like an unexpected firecracker or surprise birthday party, are not necessarily coincidences. So a surprising and improbable coincidence captures attention and seems to demand explanation.

People use the word *coincidence* in two starkly opposing ways: either as attention worthy or as irrelevant. Adjectives used with the word *coincidence* sharpen the direction of the intended meaning. When coincidences are thought to be important or to have a cause, the speaker will use adjectives such as "meaningful," "remarkable," or "amazing." One might say: "That was an amazing coincidence." When the coincidence is viewed as irrelevant, as due to chance, adjectives such as "mere," "only," "pure," "sheer," and "just" will modify the word. "That's just a coincidence." And when the word is used without a modifying adjective, the speaker's intended meaning may be unclear: "It was a coincidence that you showed up when I did." In this and my previous books, the word *coincidence* is usually intended to mean meaningful coincidence.

One thing about coincidences is certain—they are all around us. In our daily lives, on the internet, social media, radio, movies, and with each other. They are part of the fabric of our Earth-bound reality.

Four Types
The phrase *meaningful coincidence* is an umbrella term that covers four words used to describe various types of meaningful coincidence: synchronicity, serendipity, seriality, and simulpathity. The definitions of these four words overlap.

Synchronicity tends to be used for interpersonal, psychological, and spiritual coincidences. *Serendipity* (also known as happy accidents) tends to be used for finding useful ideas, things, people, and information in unexpected ways. Both synchronicity and serendipity usually involve a match between a mental event and an environmental event. *Seriality* tends to refer to coincidence-involving elements that can be observed by anyone, like seeing the same number repeated, like 1111. *Simulpathity* usually involves the simultaneous experience, akin to telepathy, of the pain or distress of a loved one who is someplace else.

General Explanations

The recognition of similarity between two events requires someone to notice the similarity. Noticing the similarity is fundamental to the existence of meaningful coincidences. Therefore, the primary explanation, the primary cause of a meaningful coincidence, is the conscious registering of the paired events by a conscious mind, a mind that notices and derives meaning.[1]

The two most popular explanations involve either randomness or chance and mystery, including God/Universe. These two explanations cannot both be right since they are opposites. They share the belief that human agency has nothing to do with creating meaningful coincidences. But as you will see, our own actions have a good deal to do with creating many of the meaningful coincidences in our lives.

While many people prefer a single explanation for coincidences like randomness or God, the more comprehensive approach includes these two and your own capacity for decision-making, each influencing the outcome to varying degrees. Your preferred explanation is built upon your ontology, from your basic beliefs about how reality works. Either we live in a random universe or God is the source of everything. What is your preferred explanation? Each coincidence has a probability of happening so randomness/chance plays a part. But many synchronicities are hard to explain, invoking mystery.

Synchronicities provide clues to how reality works, and they highlight the function of the psychosphere. Ideas that help explain how synchronicities work include fractals, complexity theory, morphic resonance, quantum fields, and the Human Global Positioning

---

1. Beitman, Bernard, "Psychology Influences the Perception of Synchronicity," *Psychology Today* website, November 3, 2023.

System (GPS).[2] Our learning about reality will keep expanding through the hints provided by meaningful coincidences.

Their Usefulness

Meaningful coincidences can be practical. They may confirm that you are on the right path. This English nursery rhyme told many children that apparently random actions can result in a good feeling about yourself.

> *Little Jack Horner*
> *Sat in the corner,*
> *Eating his Christmas pie;*
> *He put in his thumb,*
> *And pulled out a plum,*
> *And said, "What a good boy am I!"*

You may need something, and it shows up, providing you with vitally needed money, job opportunities, medical information, or spiritual direction. These happy accidents often take place by being in the right place at the right time, like sitting next to a stranger who ends up being helpful. Coincidences can help with decision-making and can show you how you are connected with other people, plants, animals, and the Earth itself. They can illuminate your own undiscovered abilities, especially the wide-ranging capacities of your intuition.

Sometimes they are simply a lot of fun. They can make you feel that you are being touched by an angel or being entertained by a stand-up comic.

How to Increase the Frequency of Coincidences

A fundamental message of this book: Keep a coincidence diary! The more you see coincidences, the more you will see. Curiosity drives

---

2. Bernard Beitman, *Meaningful Coincidences: How and Why Synchronicity and Serendipity Happen* (Rochester, VT: Park Street Press, 2022).

increases in meaningful coincidences, especially disruptive, proactive, searching actions that lead to unintended consequences. These unintended consequences sometimes take the form of serendipity and synchronicity. Searching can disturb networks of connections we know little about until aspects of that network are revealed when we shake them up with searching curiosity.[3]

The primary "cause" of a meaningful coincidence is noticing it. As obvious as that sounds, if you don't see it, for you it does not exist, it did not happen. So you have to believe that they happen *and* that they can be useful to you in some way. If they can't be useful, why notice them? Being in the right place and at the right time is not enough; you must make the connection between your need and the external event for it to be labeled a meaningful coincidence. Then act on it.

Being in the Now is key. Pay attention to your attention. After you notice the potential in a situation, be ready to act.

Since your ability to notice them is the primary cause of coincidences, your personality characteristics influence how many and what kinds you will notice. If you are curious, open to both your internal and external worlds, and/or like to find and match patterns, you are likely to see more coincidences. Also being spiritual or religious, searching for meaning in life, and being intuitive increase your coincidence frequency. Being self-referential, which means you easily connect external events with your mental activity, also makes you more likely to see coincidences.[4]

How you move through your life matters. Lying in bed, staring at the ceiling, and hoping something meaningful will happen is unlikely to result in what you are imagining coming true. Since coincidences involve intersections between two or more events, the greater the number of intersections in your life, the more synchronicities will happen. Moving around in a stimulus-rich environment will more likely create

---

3. Pievani, T., *Serendipity: The Unexpected in Science.* (London: MIT Press, 2024)
4. To estimate your coincidence sensitivity, find the Weird Coincidence Survey linked at coincider.com.

matching patterns for you to notice. An old saying advises: *the dog that trots about finds the bone*, to which I add, *especially near a butcher shop*. Keep moving, especially in places where what you need is likely to be found. This saying guides my actions as you will see.

Breaking out of regular daily patterns opens the doors of novelty. Alter your states of consciousness with meditation, travel, getting lost, trying new things, meeting new people, going to dances, and using mind-altering substances. Romance is a hotbed of coincidences. During major life stressors like birth, marriage, death of a loved one, job changes, and health challenges, coincidences are also more likely to pop up. Take a chance on chance!

Tell your friends and acquaintances your coincidence stories. Ask them about theirs. When another person is involved with your coincidence, ask them about their perspective on it. If you are perplexed by a synchronicity, ask someone you respect for their input about it.

Hone your intuition; it sends you messages in three primary ways—gut urges, heart emotions, and the still, small voice. Try to determine which urges, feelings, and voices are associated with positive, negative, and neutral outcomes. Hearing voices is not necessarily a sign of psychiatric illness.[5] The still, small voice you hear can be a remarkable guide for you.

Learn from negative and failed coincidences. If negative—for whom was it negative? Often someone else is involved. What can you learn about how you interpreted the coincidence, or how you decided to act? What does this negative outcome tell you about which intuitive channel needs more honing? Try to follow the consequences of a negative-outcome coincidence. Sometimes they turn out to be quite positive in the long run.

My Hope
Current scientific research will continue to explore the tiniest and largest mysteries of our expanding universe. The biggest mystery for us is

---

5. Bernard D. Beitman, "On Hearing Voices," Psychology Today website, August 8, 2022.

the human mind-heart and its relationship to our surroundings. The range of coincidences points at innate human capacities that connect us to each other, the natural world, and something greater. Synchronicity, serendipity, seriality, and simulpathity can be instrumental in helping us find our life's purpose and to connect with others with similar purposes.

I hope you find the love that nourishes us all. Keep your childlike curiosity active. I believe that science will one day grasp the potential of studying meaningful coincidences so that humanity may more successfully utilize them to mitigate our destructive urges and increase loving connections. But there are downsides to almost everything on this planet. Not everyone will be able to participate in the expanding awareness of our interconnectedness.

The Structure of This Book

I am the founder of The Coincidence Project. Our mission is to encourage people around the world to tell each other coincidence stories. In this and other ways we hope to make synchronicity part of world culture. This book offers a model for writing Coincidence Diaries. Most lives are filled with coincidences because coincidences help create the story line for each of our lives. "No coincidence, no story" is true for narrative fiction; it is also true for the story of our lives. A life without coincidences may be a life unlived. A coincidence diary is the story of your life.

Each story in this book is accompanied by a comment (doctor's note) and a principle. These comments and principles emerge from my decades-long study of thousands of stories, two previous coincidence books, an extensive knowledge of psychotherapy, and an academic research background. I hope that these comments and principles will encourage you to think about your own coincidences and to consider principles by which they may be used and understood. As you read through this lifetime collection, I encourage you to record the synchronicities that you remember as well as to record new ones. Coincidences are like dreams, easy to forget. And like some unexamined dreams, they are like letters you did not open.

So become open to coincidences. Coincidences are a reality show—they show us reality. My story progresses from a deep sense of isolation as a child to increasing immersion in the interconnections of all the beings here on Earth.

PART 1

Coincidence in Place

The first part of this book is largely divided into the places I have lived, which has usually involved a school in the area. I spent the years from age five to age sixty-nine being "institutionalized." I start with elementary school and go through junior and senior high school, medical school, internship and residency, two years in the United States Public Health Service, ten years at the University of Washington, and twenty-four years at the University of Missouri-Columbia, and in Charlottesville, Virginia, since 2009. I am a recovering academic who strives to be systematic about synchronicities and serendipities.

1
Shaker Heights

THE CHILD SHAPES THE ADULT. So please allow me to introduce the very young Bernie to you.

My parents, Karl Beitman and Anne Behr barely knew each other in Germany, although they had friends in common. They separately fled the Nazi terror and met at the wedding of my mother's sister and father's friend in Wilmington, Delaware, in 1939. Several of my relatives

Brother Allen and Bernie with parents Anne and Karl, Detroit, Michigan. I'm sitting next to my mother.

were killed by Nazis, including my Uncle Hans Julius and my cousins Bernhard, Achim Allen, and Marion. Their names are inscribed on a wall in Wiesbaden near where the synagogue once stood. They live on in my genes. After Karl and Anne were married, they moved to Detroit, Michigan, where I was born in 1942. My brother Allen was born there in 1943. We are "Irish twins" because our births are separated by only sixteen months. As teenagers, some people mixed us up.

When I was three, we moved to Shaker Heights, Ohio, into a duplex on the outskirts of this fancy Cleveland neighborhood. Soon after arriving, I went outside and sat on the curb of Menlo Road, watching boys playing in the street. As I write this I can feel my little boy legs, knees pointing toward the boys, feet on the street, thighs connecting with my upright body. I watched. It was a circus of movement, intriguing. They invited me to play with them. The game, I learned later, was called football. It became a love of my life.

AWARE OF BEING AWARE

At age four, I began to talk for the first time. My first words were *Magic Chef*, which was the brand of stove we had. The emblem was at my eye level. Delayed speaking is a sign of Asperger's.

Sometimes, while lying in my bed looking at the ceiling, my mother thought I was depressed. I wasn't. I was watching the thoughts flowing through my mind.

Doctor's Notes

At age four, I became aware of the self-observer of my mind, a key aspect of synchronicity awareness.

Principle

Ongoing awareness of meaningful coincidences relies on our ability to step back from similar paired events to wonder about them. This means first noticing that two apparently independent events are surprisingly similar. Some people have a "coincidence alert button" in their minds that signals awareness of an odd pairing of similarity.

Under the scrutiny of the self-observer, the thinking mind generates questions. "What are the chances of this happening?" "What does it mean for me personally?" "What does it suggest about how reality works?"

AN EXISTENTIAL MOMENT AT CAMP

In second grade I went to overnight camp on Lake Erie near some pine forests. We slept on beds in a long, narrow one-story building with showers and toilets at one end. One day they sent me to the infirmary, thinking I was sick. I was put in a bed with tall railings like a big crib. A day or two later, they let me out. I walked back to the dormitory. When I got back to the bunkhouse, nobody asked where I had been or in any way acknowledged my return. The campers' lives had gone on as if I weren't there, and then I was there—or was I? It seemed like death. I was an invisible person who was returning to the life I had once led. I didn't seem to exist except in my own mind. I got back into the routine.

📝 Doctor's Notes

This experience of my own isolation, of my social invisibility, increased my capacity to observe my mental activities and to subsequently learn to connect events in my surroundings to my mental activities, forming the basis of coincidence sensitivity.

Principle

The only reality some of us know is the functioning of our mind. Meaningful coincidences can draw us out of ourselves into the world around us. This early life moment had me believing that I was separate and isolated. But no, the similarities between psychological events and external events repeatedly show us that we are not isolated. We are also deeply embedded in our social and natural worlds.

SNAPPER

Being caught up in my own mind left me lonely. I needed a companion. My father brought home a one-year-old dog with whom I found no connection. The dog was returned to the original owner. Then he brought home a two-week-old puppy who vomited blood and died. I went around the house in deep anguish, saying to my parents: "You killed my dog. You killed my dog." Soon my father brought home a six-week-old puppy. He was black with tan and white splotches and liked to chew on trees (he was teething). I named him Snapper.

We became best buddies. We'd go behind the garage where I mixed liquids in the garbage like pickle juice and ketchup. I would sniff them and then Snapper would sniff them. He was interested. While we were waiting in the car for my mother to come out of the doctor's office, I showed him how to jump through the open car window onto the seat. After a few tries, he got it down. We both enjoyed his success. I petted him and he smiled.

Snapper, brother Allen, and Bernie, Wilmington, Delaware.

One day when I was about eight or nine years old, Snapper was not home when I came back from elementary school. I asked my mother where he was. She didn't know and suggested I go to the police station near my elementary school. I rode my bike the usual route to school, cut across the playground, crossed the big street, and pushed the bike up the stairs, and then took the long walk to the front of the police station. I pushed open the big doors. A big man in uniform sat behind the large entrance desk. "Have you seen my dog?" He shook his head, "Sorry, son, we haven't seen your dog." Tears flooded my eyes as I left. I wasn't paying attention to where I was going. I went down the stairs. But instead of recrossing the big street, I pedaled on the sidewalk on the right side of the street. Sobbing, sobbing, sobbing. Then I looked up and there, coming toward me, was a black dog walking in Snapper's sideways style. Could it be? Could it be? Yes! It was Snapper! He was casually happy to see me, jumping up on my legs, letting me pet his head. He seemed to be asking me why I'd taken so long to find him.

🗒 Doctor's Notes

I was reunited with my best friend. I call this coincidence type "Human GPS." It's also known as being in the "right place, right time" or getting where you need to be, guided by intuition. We humans and our dogs have the ability to path-find, something like GPS in cars. This highly meaningful coincidence for the lonely boy that I was set me on the trail of coincidences.

Principles

Getting lost can create highly meaningful coincidences.
What you are seeking may also be seeking you.

SHARED GRIEF

In 2021, three friends, Juliet, Peter, and Patrick, gathered with me for a memorial for Snapper. I read a eulogy for him.

Dear Snapper,

 You were the first person I could relate to, to love and feel love from you. I remember us sitting up the hill over River Road in Wilmington. You sat there, with your head turned toward me, listening. Our friends know the coincidence of us finding each other. They don't know that Pop had you killed when I was fourteen. They did not tell me until I was twenty-one. I blamed myself for you growling at the little kids pulling your tail. Maybe I was not paying enough attention to you because of girls and football and baseball. I miss you still, but today you are helping put the past into the past. All those raw feelings about Anne and Karl Beitman so long ago are fading. I left home in 1960 for college and came home for three summers but hardly had anything to do with them. They were strangers almost. I guess they did not know how to relate to me, and me to them. They tried with what they had.

 You were loving, steadfast, and true. I honor your memory. This is like the Commandment to Honor thy Father and thy Mother.

 You seemed to have nightmares while you were snoozing. I liked when you licked my toes. You were my best friend ever. I liked barking with you.

 I liked going through the garbage with you.

 I was upset when Pop had to spank you for pooping in the living room, but I thought it was funny too. What were you mad about?

 Now with my friends around, I am able to bury you and with this act say goodbye to so much trauma and tears and fears in my distant and recent past.

 Goodbye my friend!

Then Juliet told the story of how her father said her dog was killed by a car. Years later she found out that her father had taken the dog someplace else. The Snapper funeral became a dual funeral for her dog and mine. Later that day, Peter told us that his father had secretly removed his dog from the home and for a long time never told him.

🗒 Doctor's Notes

Three of the four people at Snapper's memorial had similar experiences with their father and their dog.

Snapper influenced the creation of two coincidences. One early in his life and the other decades after his death at his memorial service. My father sometimes said in German, *Der Hund lacht*—"The dog is smiling." I hope he still is.

Dogs are popular family members, and our fathers have their reasons. My father was an immigrant who feared the authorities as he had in Germany. He was afraid he would be sued if Snapper injured a child. The three of us could share together the emptiness created by our fathers and fill the void a little bit by sharing our grief together.

--- **Principle** ---

Your seemingly unique experience is probably not unique to you. I was not the only child whose father had taken their beloved dog. Meaningful coincidences often share dual aspects—augmenting our own sense of uniqueness and showing us the deep similarity with many other human beings. To have that idea driven home at the same time makes this principle more starkly real.

2
Wilmington

ELEMENTARY SCHOOL AND HIGH SCHOOL offered several being-in-the-right-place-at-the-right-time serendipities, each requiring the need to act.

PRESIDENT OF THE STUDENT COUNCIL

Near the end of fifth grade, our family moved to Wilmington, Delaware, so that my mother could rejoin her mother and three sisters and their families. There were only two weeks left of fifth grade at my new school, Edgemoor Elementary, and my brother Allen and I missed most of them because we had picked blackberries in a field of poison ivy.

For the first time at my new school, there would be an election for student council president. Any sixth grader could run. The Moreland Elementary School in Shaker Heights had well-established campaign methods that I would use as part of my Edgemoor campaign. I tapped Jimmy Foulkes to play his saxophone for "Bernie Beitman for President." He got a few other players to join, forming a band. We paraded from classroom window to classroom window of the one-story building. While they played songs like "America the Beautiful," I stood in front of them beaming and smiling into the darkened classrooms.

I also put up a poster folded in half. On the front I wrote,

Open this poster and you will see
Who is voting for Bernie B.

23

When they opened the poster, they looked into a mirror. They saw themselves.

The new boy won the election!

📝 Doctor's Notes

What does it take to make something you want happen? Luck is when opportunity meets preparation. Was I lucky? Yes. But I had to seize the opportunity. I was prepared by having observed well-established election campaigning methods, remembering them, and applying them.

Principle

Being in the right place at the right time may not be enough. I will repeat this emphasis on agency. You have to act to seize the moment. The time window in which action leads to desired results can vary from thirty seconds to hours, sometimes a day or two, perhaps even longer. You can create a meaningful coincidence by putting two incidents together yourself.

THE WIZARD OF OZ

Later that sixth-grade year, my class put on a puppet show of *The Wizard of Oz*. Someone, probably one of the teachers, asked me to be the Wizard. I didn't know the story. Toto, Dorothy's dog, pulls back the curtain of the Mighty Oz to reveal a gentleman pulling a lot of levers to create the light-and-sound show that had made the Wizard famous and scary. I never knew who or why I was asked to play this role. But it fit me perfectly. Here's why.

As the first student council meeting gathered, all eyes were on me, including the eyes of Mrs. Hall. Looking back, I think they all thought that because I had run such a marvelous campaign, I also knew how to run a student council meeting. While, yes, I had been a student council representative in the previous elementary school, I did not pay attention to the meetings. They were boring. I looked out the window a lot. I had no idea how to run a student council meeting. I remember nothing after the deafening, empty silence.

I had enacted a metaphor of the Wizard of Oz. All lights and sound. No substance. Even as a sixth grader I recognized the ironic parallel.

📝 Doctor's Notes

Since I didn't know the teacher's intention behind asking me to be the Wizard, it became a meaningful coincidence. Maybe Mrs. Hall had something to do with it. If you know the cause of a coincidence, then it is no longer a coincidence since a coincidence is defined as having no clear explanation. Here the explanation would be a teacher's intention to reflect myself back to myself. Or maybe they just needed someone to play the role. Or maybe there was information floating around in the localized psychosphere of Edgemoor Elementary School that a teacher subconsciously registered.

What a great lesson! Since then, I have tried to have more substance in the roles I play. It was another step in the progression of my recognizing that my mind is embedded in my surroundings.

Principle

Your mind can be mirrored in your environment. How it happens is a source of endless curiosity. That it happens is a fact of life on this planet. If you expect mirroring, then you are more likely to see it and be able to learn from it.

THE LITTLE LEAGUE ALL-STAR TEAM

In Shaker Heights, I played on our elementary school summer baseball team against other elementary schools. We had no uniforms or playoffs or anything actually organized. In Wilmington I discovered Little League baseball. The real thing! Hurray! So my father drove my brother Allen and me to tryouts. To my amazement, we were going to play in a real professional baseball stadium, home of the Wilmington minor league baseball team. As we came to the end of the upper tunnel through the stands, I was greeted with the most beautiful sight. All over the field were kids throwing balls and batting and running around on this real-life baseball diamond just like on television. Oh my! We walked down onto the field and showed the coaches what we could do. Later we were assigned to various teams. My coach was Frannie Fortunata, and our assistant coach was Mr. Dean. I got to play short-stop and bat fourth, both key positions. Allen was assigned to a team in the other league so we never played against each other.

I made the All-Star team. We traveled what seemed to be a great distance across the Delaware Memorial Bridge into Penns Grove, New Jersey, where, for the first time, I saw a real Little League field, sized for us nine- to twelve-year-olds. (Our Wilmington field was the infield of the pros.) I batted seventh, struck out at least once, and got no hits. I was disoriented in this new location. We went home as losers, and that was the end of All-Star baseball for me.

🗒 Doctor's Notes

In the new city, I needed organized baseball. I checked around, asked kids, and voila, my need was realized. I'd never heard of Little League. Why did I need organized baseball? It had more challenges than pickup games. My body called out for the challenge of athletic competition, for chances to keep improving, and to excel.

Principle

Keep looking for something and you may surprise yourself by unex-pectedly finding it. Serendipity often involves looking for something and finding it in unexpected ways. Here I was looking for something I did not even know existed.

THREE GIRLS ASK ME TO RANK THEM

One day in eighth grade I came out of my house on the way to play baseball. Three girls were waiting for me. I was surprised! What are they doing here?

They asked me who I liked best. I replied, "Diane first, Randy second, Phyllis third. Please excuse me, I'm going to play baseball."

📑 Doctor's Notes

To me this was a meaningful coincidence. Three girls I liked wanting to know who I liked in what order!!! Appearing outside my house!!! With the necessary timing for me to meet them?

Coincidences often trigger, "What are the odds of that happening?" This was an unexpected, surprising, low-probability event. Looking back, I can try to explain this surprising event. Even though they lived in different neighborhoods at least a mile apart, they must have planned this event and executed it. Three thirteen-year-old girls agreeing on the intention to be ranked by me is also a low-probability event.

Principle

Some coincidences can have explanations even though the explanations are also unlikely. Their planning and executing was an improbable event.

A PAST-LIFE MEMORY?

An image haunted my teenage mind. I was running out of a wooden barracks at what seemed like a Nazi concentration camp, at night, toward a barbed wire fence. I jumped on the fence and began climbing, impervious to the barbs tearing my flesh. I knew what would happen, and it did. Spotlights crawled over me as I reached for the top of the fence. Machine guns ripped holes in me. I was left hanging on the fence, dead.

Why? The next thought I had was, I would never be able to see my girlfriend again. The anguish of never being with her was too much to bear. That is why I committed suicide.

Now, in this life, when I wash scraps of food from my plate, I pretend and wish I could give those scraps to the starving people in the barracks of that Nazi concentration camp.

I notice several thought patterns that seem to be eerily similar to what drove me to that imagined/remembered suicide: (1) No one can help me. (2) I will sacrifice myself for love. (3) People and things will be taken from me. (4) I will continue to harm myself.

📝 Doctor's Notes

Are these "real" memories? I was born in 1942 in the middle of the Holocaust. My parents never talked about the terror and death, although I was named after a murdered cousin, as was my brother, Allen. Did I pick up those images from my parents and come to believe they were my own?

What if I told you that I have met that girlfriend in this life? Would you believe me? How would I know it was her? By the love for her that poured out of my heart when we first met and held hands. And the love I felt for her for years afterward. She has named me her spiritual grandfather. We keep in touch.

Principle

Evidence continues to accumulate that many of us have had previous lives. Here was a visionary hint that I too have had at least one past life. Have you?

A TEAMMATE BECOMES
PRESIDENT OF THE UNITED STATES

After playing in that fantastic minor league baseball stadium, the Wilmington Little League moved to a real Little League stadium. But I was thirteen and the age limit was twelve, so my brother Allen could play and I couldn't. I sadly, enviously, watched him play.

Fortunately, baseball-loving coaches formed a Babe Ruth league so that at age fourteen, I could not only play on a regular-size field, but Allen and I could play on the same team. For each game, box scores in the local newspaper listed the players, the order they batted in, how many times they batted, and how many hits they had, among other things. Two of those box scores had the name Biden on them. I still have a team photo with Joe Biden's signature on it.

📝 Doctor's Notes

Knowing this very friendly "average Joe" who became president inspired me to continue to expand coincidence work.

———————————————— **Principle** ————————————————

Famous people must be known by not-famous people. It has to happen. Joe has met many, many people. I'm just one who had the fortune to be near him for a while. Who are you close to who might also inspire you to greater heights?

HOW TO WIN THE BATTING TITLE

As a ninth grader on the baseball team, Coach Elmer Fennick let me bat maybe four times. No hits. In tenth grade, I played second base a few times and batted about .150, or two hits out of thirteen at bats (.300 is a good batting average). The next year, our new coach John Michaelwicz showed me how to drag bunt, which involved fooling the third baseman into thinking I was going to swing when instead, at the last moment, I stuck the bat out and the ball dribbled down the third base line. Then I sprinted to first base. I got seventeen hits out of thirty-five at bats my junior year, seven of which were drag bunts. I won the batting title at .486 and was selected for the All-Conference first team.

📝 Doctor's Notes

Sometimes the right person shows up at the right time. Mr. Michaelwicz was serendipity personified. I wasn't looking for him. He showed up, saw the potential in me, and trained me to do what he knew how to do. Had he not had that skill to teach, there would have been no batting title for Bernie.

———————————————— **Principle** ————————————————

The right people may come into your life at the right time. Get ready to accept their help!

A POWER PARTNERSHIP

In tenth grade, I bought a red-and-white-striped newsboy flat cap with a button to firm down the cap to the brim. Maybe I did it to be fashionable, or maybe to standout, or probably because I thought it was fun somehow. And lo and behold, there was another guy in the hallway at school with the same hat! Had I subconsciously seen it on him? Or did he see it on me? Neither of us remembered seeing the hat on the other person's head until we both ran into each other and were startled by the mirroring. Bob Warner and I became best friends wearing the striped hat.

We plotted to lead the student council, ran as co-presidents, and handily won. We conducted the meetings together, organized events, and secured an orange drink machine to make cash for the student council. And we talked about girls a lot.

We helped each other through some rough spots of adulthood and are still friends. Each time we talk by phone, he threatens to visit me from New Hampshire. Will he? And it's hard to find replicas of those hats.

📝 Doctor's Notes

Independent purchases of stand-out hats coincidentally brought us together for a lifelong friendship. We each needed a best friend, were very good students, loved sports, and were ambitious. How did we know to signal each other in this way? I don't know. Another fruitful coincidence with an unknown explanation. (I like to think each of us has a spirit guide helping us along the path.)

Principle

Finding a mirror of an aspect of yourself in another person invariably drives curiosity. Investigate? Or investigate! Meaningful coincidences can serve as suggestions, not commands. Use your intuition to decide whether to wonder and then wander into new territory.

TRYING OUT FOR PITTSBURG PIRATES

Tom Paton, one of the top two pitchers on our baseball team and a tough lineman on the football team, had a car. We decided to watch a game at Joe Biden's high school. *This was the only time we went to a game together.* As the game wore on, I noticed one of the coaches pointing toward Tom and me. Another man followed the direction the coach was pointing. He came up to us and pulled out a newspaper article with the headline announcing that Beitman had won the batting title. He asked if that was me. He invited me to come to a Pittsburg Pirates tryout camp. And because Tom was a big strong guy, he got invited too. At the tryout, we ran around, fielded, and tried to hit. The pitcher I was matched against threw the ball so fast, it was like swinging at aspirins. After a few hours, we went home.

📝 Doctor's Notes

We were in the right place at the right time to be noticed, asked, and then secure bragging rights—"I tried out for the Pittsburg Pirates." Tom and I were not especially good friends. I suggest that our internal Human GPS might have aided the decision to go to this game together.

Principle

The dog that trots about finds the bone. Keep moving and perhaps interesting and useful or fun things will happen.

FALLING IN LOVE WITH MY FOOTBALL SELF

After two years on the Junior Varsity team, as a senior, I finally made first team on the Varsity team at left halfback. Toward the end of the first game, I ran a counterplay for fifty yards that sealed the victory. Two days later, on a Monday afternoon, the coaches herded the team to sit on the auditorium stage. No one was in the audience. They then showed us the film of that game. I saw myself making this clever run and fell in love with that beautiful image of the fluid, intelligent, and focused runner that was me. I was twelve feet tall on the screen and in my mind.

📝 Doctor's Notes

Is this a coincidence? For me, it was. We can explain it looking back. The coaches decided, planned, and did it. Yet it was a dramatic, unexpected surprise to me and so became a meaningful coincidence. It was the only time the coaches showed us film in that dramatic fashion. The effect was to increase my confidence as a running back. (Was that their intention?)

Principle

Like the three girls showing up at my house, explanations become apparent. Yet to the teenager that was me, the explanations were not apparent because the surprise overwhelmed rationality. These stories suggest that in the more complex world of adulthood, reasonable explanations can be sought and discovered.

AN EXPECTED AND UNEXPECTED OPPORTUNITY

In that first football game, I sealed the victory against Wilmington High with that fifty-yard counterplay. Against P. S. DuPont, on their home field, which was very familiar to me, I made two touchdowns. And then came the battle for the conference title against Conrad. The night before, Bob Warner orchestrated a huge bonfire. On our opening drive, I scored the first touchdown of the game. On our second drive, I went about forty yards to their three-yard line. Our world-class sprinter Rod Lambert took it into the end zone. We won 40–0 in what was supposed to be a close game.

Because of these runs, I made first team All-Conference. Foolishly and honestly, I sent a letter to the sports columnist of the local paper saying that Lambert should have been selected because he was more valuable. Since the all the conference coaches vote for the All-Conference players, I was saying I knew better. A teenage humble-brag?

Because we went 9–0, our coaches were selected to coach the North in the Delaware All-Star game. They could pick no more than six players from our team. They did not pick me. I was mad. Then I noticed a newspaper article saying that our center had to leave early for football camp with the Navy. So I walked up to the high school, found the coaches, and told them I wanted to play. They said they thought I did not want to play because of the letter I sent to the newspaper. Really? I didn't believe them. They did let me replace our center.

📝 Doctor's Notes

The unexpected departure of our center created an opening for me to run through. Finding openings while running with the football is essential for a good running back. Experience, desire, intuition, calmness, and visual scanning each play a part in finding the opening. Then quick action must follow.

—————— **Principle** ——————

Be ready to move when the opening appears. Scan your environment for openings by first believing that openings will appear. Then calmly and quickly step on through!

3
Swarthmore

JUST FIFTEEN MILES FROM MY HOME in Wilmington, Swarthmore College was small enough for my 5'10", 160-pound body to play college football. Three upper classmen in high school whom I deeply respected, and who went there, added to the recommendation. The University of Delaware was my other choice. Looking back, I could have applied to fancy schools like Penn State or Brown or Yale or Duke, but no one had suggested any other places. During my senior year at Swarthmore, I was touring with a possible freshman who mentioned that he was considering either Harvard or Swarthmore. Only then did I realize I was attending a fancy small college, ranked number three in the nation at that time. Surprise!

NUMBER 23

A teammate wanted #26 for his football jersey, so I traded him for #23. I didn't care; #44, my high school number, was not available. So like an old-fashioned billboard carrier or the huge number of T-shirts with ads on them, I broadcast #23.

It became my number out in the world, seeming to appear in unexpected places, doing for me what numbers often do for people, reassuring me that I was on the right path.

On August 23, 1965, a new girlfriend and I were hitchhiking back to Los Angeles from San Francisco. We received two rides going south on Highway 101 and then another ride over to Monterey, then another ride down the Pacific Coast Highway, with a stop at the Hearst Castle where we got a ride into to Los Angeles. We received 5 rides: 2 + 3. Our last drivers invited us to their apartment. It was number 23.

📝 Doctor's Notes

At the University of Missouri–Columbia, the Weird Coincidence Survey asked participants if they liked some numbers better than others. At the time, no numbers seemed to stand out. Since then, "angel numbers" have become increasingly popular, the favorite being 1111 especially the time on digital clocks 11:11. Also, other repeated numbers like 2:22 and 3:33 are accompanied by reports of waking up and seeing this matching pair of numbers.

The number 23 gets a lot of attention. We humans have 23 pairs of chromosomes in our genetic makeup. The number 23 is used in at least two movies. *The Number 23* focuses on a book that seemingly mirrors the protagonist's own life. The movie entitled *23* focuses on the protagonist's obsession with the number 23.[1] In the early 1900s, the phrase "23 skidoo" became a popular slang expression; "23" and skidoo each came to mean "leave quickly." In chapter 23 of Aleister Crowley's *Book of Lies,* he describes the number 23 as meaning "Get OUT." To get OUT meant to leave all patterns behind and go beyond your group norms and rules.[2]

John Nash, the central person in the movie *A Beautiful Mind,* found 23 to be his favorite prime number.[3]

--- **Principle** ---

Find your number! There may very well be one for you. There are so many numbers around us every day that once you select your number, you are likely to find it everywhere around you. The most

1. "The Number 23," Wikipedia website; "23 (film)," Wikipedia website.
2. Aleister Crowley, *The Book of Lies,* chap. 23 (London: Wieland, 1913), 55.
3. Patrick J. Kiger, "What's the Fascination with Number 23?," HowStuff Works website, June 9, 2023.

useful thing about number coincidences is that they make you wonder about what might be behind them. Activating curiosity about meaningful coincidences is central to exploring them.

A HEBREW LETTER TOUCHDOWN

During my second autumn at Swarthmore in 1961, I ran the opening kickoff of the second half for a ninety-seven-yard return against one of our archrivals, Pennsylvania Military College. We were the intellectual wimps; they were the muscle men, just three miles away. I had often imagined running an open kickoff back for a touchdown. This was the second time. It's a great feeling—one of my very favorite things to do. The video of the film of that run is on my website.

Later, during my internship in San Francisco in 1968–69, I thought about the pattern of that run as I was studying tarot cards. Each of the

Senior Year at Swarthmore, Swarthmore, PA.

Left to *right*, Early Hebrew, Middle Hebrew, Late Hebrew, and Modern Hebrew lamed.

major trumps is associated with one of the twenty-two Hebrew letters. The run pattern strongly resembles the shape of the twelfth letter in the Hebrew alphabet, lamed. The Early Hebrew letters were pictographs of common images in the surroundings. Aleph, the first letter, represented an ox, and beth, the second letter, represented a house. Lamed represented an ox goad or a shepherd's staff used to direct sheep by pushing or pulling them. It was also used as a weapon against predators to defend and protect the sheep. Another meaning of *lamed* is "toward," as in moving something like oxen and sheep in a specific direction. The letter came to mean authority, as it is a sign of the shepherd, the leader of the flock.[4] More symbolically it can mean teacher. I ran the Modern Hebrew lamed starting from the bottom of the letter. My primary deviation from the current lamed shape was the top line. I bent it to the left. I got tired.

With the ball in my hands, on the canvas of the football field, did I draw a symbol of my future?

📝 Doctor's Notes

Why was I replaying this touchdown in the movie theater of my mind while living in a cinder-block room off the garage of a house in the Berkeley, California, hills? Back by popular demand? I had once been a big man on campus. Now I had no such role as a medical intern. The memory comforted me and also connected me firmly to tarot cards and meaningful coincidences. The cards seem to mirror reality.

Principle

Our actions can be symbolic predictions of our future.

---

4. Jeff A. Benner, "Lamed," Ancient Hebrew Research Center website.

LIBRARY ANGEL

With time on my hands, I strolled through the stacks in the basement of the library at Swarthmore. Could I find something interesting? Somehow, a thin book with a green cover and some white caught my attention. The title was even more enticing: *A Theory of Personality* (1963) by Ohio State psychologist George Kelly. Kelly's key idea was "A person's processes are psychologically channelized by the way he anticipates events." A simpler way to say this is, *expectations strongly influence experience.* I reread the first chapter many times trying to squeeze out some of the meaning. It was difficult, but I stayed with it. Little did I know then that this little book was going to be the key to my medical school thesis and the key that unlocked a slot in the psychiatric residency program at Stanford.

📝 Doctor's Notes

A common coincidence involves raising a question and having it answered in an unexpected way through a book, TV, radio, or the internet. Many people report a book falling off the shelf of a bookstore or library or even in someone's house right onto the floor in front of them. Or the book seems to attract your attention in some mysterious way. One person saw a book that to her was a flashing light. And it turns out to be just the right book. It was a valuable find for me!

Principle

Library and internet angels can flutter into your vision. Be alert to the sound of their wings.

PRECOGNITION THROUGH ACTION

Later that fall, on the Thursday before we played Johns Hopkins, I went on automatic pilot. I was moved by an intention outside my conscious mind. I walked away from the football practice field to an adjacent field, got two tackling dummies, and placed them next to each other with a little space between them. I picked up a football, walked about ten yards from the dummies, turned around, crouched, tucked the ball between my arms, quickly turned back around, and sprinted between the two dummies. I repeated this pattern once, and then trotted back to the practice field.

On Saturday, I was getting frustrated because the Johns Hopkins punter kept kicking the ball short so I could not catch and return it. Then, finally, he kicked a good one. I heard the loudspeaker announcer excitedly describing this great kick. To catch it, I had to turn around and catch it over my shoulder. I turned around, and there, just like on Thursday, two players were running next to each other right at me. I sprinted between them and went ninety yards for the score.

📝 Doctor's Notes

I was not surprised after catching the punt and turning around. I was prepared to sprint between the two "dummies." Each probably thought the other one was going to tackle me. This precognition through action resembles the lamed ninety-seven-yard kick-off return that predicted my future as a leader.

Principle

This pairing of two events suggests not only that we have the capacity to see the future but also that we can create a plan for what to do about it.

PARANOID AT THE LIBRARY?

The week after making three touchdowns against Johns Hopkins, I was walking out of the DuPont Science Library. I had the feeling there were people coming after me, trying to hurt me. It was a quiet November evening. I looked around. Were they on the shadow side of the building? I looked. No one was there. So I went back to my dorm and did not think much about it.

On Saturday we were again playing our archrivals, Pennsylvania Military College. As a sophomore, I had run that ninety-seven-yard kickoff return against them. As a junior, I ran into their backfield, disrupting a lateral toss from the quarterback to their running back. It embarrassed the runner and made them lose ten or fifteen yards. To my surprise, on our first offensive play of the game, our quarterback called a 9–0 one man out that put me way out as a wide receiver. I was ready to run my usual off tackle or end around. As I settled into position, the PMC defense called out, "Beitman is here, Beitman is here." What's with this? That had never happened before, opposing players calling out my name. That disoriented me. I went up for the pass, hit the ground without the ball, and got up groggy. I thought they had hit me hard. The film showed otherwise. I had gone up for the ball and landed on my head, so thrown off was I by their calling out my name. Sometime later, I was going end around as usual but not as alert and quick. As I planted my left leg, the same running back I had embarrassed the year before smashed his helmet into my thigh. That turned out to be the end of my college football career, even though I played some in the last game. I was limping.

📝 Doctor's Notes

Turns out they *were* after me. I had been picking up something from their practice sessions when they were probably practicing that one of their players was me—and going after the pretend Beitman. They were ready for me. Unfortunately, I lost control of myself when they called out my name. I had a mild concussion after hitting the ground and set myself up for injury by the running back I had embarrassed the year before. I had helped PMC fulfill my "paranoid" inklings.

Principle

Sometimes if you are not paranoid, you are not paying attention. The future was ambiguously being laid out for me. This time it was not clear enough for me to be ready for it.

MY MOTHER AND THE PRO-FOOTBALL SCOUT

The final game of my football career took place on Wednesday,

November 27, 1963, instead of Saturday, November 23. The date was pushed back because John F. Kennedy was assassinated on Friday, November 22. My mother was sitting in the stands near a man she did not know. He was a scout for the Oakland Raiders pro-football team. She had come to thank God that I made it through seven years of high school and college football without a serious injury. She did not know I had been injured the week before. I was hobbled and hobbling in front of the scout. The man exclaimed, "Is that Beitman!?" Limping around, I did not look like much of a runner that day. I would not have known the scout was there had my mother not sat near him.

📝 Doctor's Notes

A pro-football scout coming to a game to watch me? My mother going to a football game to watch me? Neither had ever happened. Yes, the stands were not that big and each person had to sit someplace. Yet, they were not necessarily within speaking distance. Right place, right time! Thanks, Ma!

——— Principle ———

Some coincidences are simply to be enjoyed. I can tell people I was scouted by the pro-football team the Oakland Raiders.

4
New Haven

LIFE AT SWARTHMORE COLLEGE was highly organized, tightly structured. Tight organization tends to reduce coincidence frequency.

Yale did not require us to attend classes and labs, although it was recommended. Tests were optional except the National Boards at the end of the second and fourth years. Students had to pass each board exam to move on to the third year and then to graduate.

We were also required to write a data-based thesis. They gave us summers off to do so. Every other medical school I knew of required students to attend classes and labs during the summer. The Yale faculty thought of themselves as creators of a nurturing incubator for researchers. And they still do.

However, standing outside our medical school dormitory, gazing at the hospital across the street, I felt I was without identity. I was no longer the best athlete in the school, and no longer one of the top two premedical students. No one knew me. I was off-balance and free.

KNOCKING ON A STRANGER'S DOOR

To receive financial support for summer research, Yale required a simple grant application. These summers were loose, unstructured times, ripe for coincidences. I applied and received a grant to participate in research at Mt. Sinai Hospital in Los Angeles. The $500 grant from Yale covered the costs.

In that summer of 1965, after my first year, I joined a guy driving a Volkswagen bug from New Haven, Connecticut, to Los Angeles, California. Somewhere on Route 66 near Flagstaff, Arizona, I realized that I had no place to stay in LA. It was time to improvise. I called a Swarthmore classmate for help. Rosita S. happened to know that our classmate Jim R. was living in Los Angeles. His apartment was in the back of a big house near 30th and Vermont not far from the University of Southern California. It was also located a block from the Watts district where, later that summer between August 11–16, Black residents rioted against police brutality and poverty.[1] I saw the explosions and the armored vehicles.

Jim welcomed me. We chatted. He told me that the owner of the house was a mystic. I walked up to her front door and knocked. A woman, Jean Brayton, answered. I said, "I hear you are a mystic." She said, "You are the second one." She meant that I was the second person to come to her seeking mystical knowledge and experience. The first was a dentist.

She invited me in. I told her that I had studied mysticism and Hindu philosophy in philosophy class. She said, "If you want a mystical experience, come back at midnight next Wednesday."

I did. She gave me a glass of milk with a blue liquid in the bottom. She said it was LSD. I had read about it in a 1963 article in *Look* magazine written by Harvard undergraduate Andrew Weil.[2] We spent most of the time in her living room, with about five or six other people. As dawn loomed, I was sitting in a chair gazing at my hands. They were about six inches apart. I saw streams of energy emanating from my hands. The energy bands lengthened when I moved my hands farther apart and constricted when I moved my hands closer together. I could see green and gold energy flowing between my fingers. A young woman came over to me. She guided one of her hands between my hands. Her hand acted like the prow of a boat going through waves. Her hand provided me with the more clear evidence of the reality of human energy

1. Jill A. Edy, "Watts Riots of 1965," Britannica website.
2. Andrew T. Weil, "The Strange Case of the Harvard Drug Scandal," *Look* magazine, November 5, 1963, Drug Library website.

fields. Stimulated by this observation, I continue to this day trying to understand how human energy fields operate and how they can be used.

Jean was starting a branch of the Ordo Templi Orientalis (OTO), a mystical organization based on the ideas of Aleister Crowley,[3] who was once known as the "wickedest man in the world." Through my association with Jean Brayton and her OTO, I was initiated into the study of the Kabbalah, tarot cards, and astrology, all of which prepared me for the ideas and experiences of the hippie culture of the late 1960s in San Francisco.

📝 Doctor's Notes

I was following what was in front of me, like clues to a gigantic puzzle or breadcrumbs leading the way. LSD and mysticism experiences were preludes to the hippie culture that was beginning to form. I found people, information, and psychoactive drugs I did not know I was seeking. These incidents provided me with more happy accidents of serendipity that furthered the foundation for my understanding and writing about meaningful coincidences. The OTO provided a great leap forward.

Principle

The loss of structure opens up new possibilities, especially if you keep your eyes open to notice things, if you move around and follow the hints and clues and your own intuition. You can hunt for new ideas and adventures in the coincidence jungle.

FINDING RUGBY

I really missed playing football. During the fall of my second year, I went out to the Yale football practice field looking for someone to play with. The starting quarterback happened to be there. He agreed to

---

3. Iona Cartier, "Solar Lodge," Blog About Alchemy and Great Alchemists website, August 8, 2010.

throw me some long passes. I was again in football heaven. He wished I played for Yale because his wide receivers were not as good as I was. Football was only for undergraduates. Sigh.

One of the football coaches noticed me running around out there and asked me if I wanted to play rugby. I had never heard of that game. So the following spring I tried out for the team, and for two years I started at left wing for Yale. My father had played left wing in soccer in Germany. It was great to be literally following in his footsteps.

📝 Doctor's Notes

The dog that trots about finds a bone, especially if he trots near a butcher shop. While I did not know the phrase back then, I was trotting about where something I wanted was likely to be found—a football practice field. Serendipity allowed me to repeat the rugby version of my father's soccer position and continue to run with the ball in the open field.

Principle

Keep moving, keep looking, especially in new places. You may unexpectedly find what you don't quite know you are seeking. Serendipities increase when you move through stimulus-rich environments.

PSYCHEDELIC RESEARCH

During my second year, I went to a talk by a Yale psychologist about the Good Friday experiment done by a Harvard divinity student. On Good Friday 1962, in the basement of Marsh Chapel at Boston University, ten divinity students were given psilocybin and ten were given nicotinic acid, which gives a flushed feeling so it works as an active placebo. Nine out of ten of the psilocybin participants had a mystical experience.[4]

---

4. Walter N. Pahnke, "Drugs and Mysticism," *International Journal of Parapsychology* 8, no. 2 (1966): 295–313.

The study had been conducted by Walter Pahnke whose thesis advisor was Harvard psychiatrist Gerald Klerman, who had recently moved to Yale. I knocked on Klerman's office door and told him about my LSD trips in Los Angeles. He helped set up a meeting with Pahnke who greeted me with "You are the first one." He meant the first medical student he knew who had taken a psychedelic.

Pahnke presented me with data from his second psilocybin experiment, which was done at the Massachusetts Mental Health Center where he was now a psychiatrist. Unlike the group study at the church, this experiment placed two subjects in a room with a facilitator, flowers, and music; the subjects and the facilitator were blind to whether they received placebo or psilocybin.

Another $500 grant from Yale paid the way for a summer in Cambridge and the collection of pre-existing data.

My paper, "Expectation and Experience with Psilocybin," based on this data, fulfilled the Yale thesis graduation requirement. The results suggested that expectations influenced the drug experience. Those who expected a sensory experience of magnified colors and sounds reported these experiences, sometimes with synesthesia (one sensation becomes another—sound becomes color, for example). Those who expected a psychological experience reported going back into childhood and finding possible origins of their current behavioral patterns. Those who expected mystical experiences commonly reported feelings of oneness and a deeply felt positive mood.

📓 Doctor's Notes

I "just happened" to find the talk about the Good Friday experiment. Klerman "just happened" to have moved to Yale. More happy accidents. I was looking for academic support for my LSD trip and needed to do research to graduate. The two needs came together.

--------------------------- **Principle** ---------------------------
What you expect to happen increases the likelihood of that happening.

My New Girlfriend's Parents

While working on the Pahnke data in Boston, I was living in a room near Harvard Square in Cambridge. One day I wandered into a party going on upstairs. I saw a beautiful girl with long dark hair. Somehow I got in touch with her, and we had a thing that lasted well past the summer. When Dina introduced me to her parents, they asked me what I was doing in Boston. As part of my story, I mentioned my Yale thesis advisor Gerry Klerman. Turns out Gerry was a good friend of theirs! My new girlfriend became one of two unpaid research assistants in analyzing the data.

📝 Doctor's Notes

How did that coincidence happen? I had nothing to do and went upstairs and looked around, made contact with the daughter of friends of Gerry Klerman, my thesis advisor. This coincidence was useful for my research. How did it happen? Dina told me she almost did not come. I had never gone upstairs before. Two unlikely events led to romantic attraction and back to my thesis advisor who had arranged for me to be in Boston in the first place.

Principle

We humans seem to have abilities that get us into places that demonstrate our interconnectedness and fulfill some of our needs. Learn to trust your inner guidance system by trial-and-error testing.

From Movie Star to a Psychoanalytic Princess

The 1962 psychiatry-imbued movie *David and Lisa* touched me deeply. Janet Margolin, who played Lisa, was so beautiful, so sweet, and so real. She was about my age. I fell in love with her, as did many other guys. A medical student who lived across the hall from me sent her an invitation to visit him and she accepted! Somehow I knew she was in his room. When I saw him walk to the lavatory, I knocked on his open door. There was Janet, lying on his bed. Wow! We talked about the book she was reading, and they invited me to join them for dinner in the dorm cafeteria. After a while, Janet said to me something like, "Have I got a girl for you!"

On a Saturday in the early spring of 1967 in Greenwich Village of New York City, my Boston girlfriend Dina broke up with me. The next day, brokenhearted, I visited Winnie Rosen, the person Janet wanted me to meet. I showed Winnie maps and plans for my upcoming trip around the world with a six-week stop in Dacca, East Pakistan (now Bangladesh). I had received a U.S. government grant to work at the Cholera Research Lab there. To add another layer to the coincidence, her father was a past president of the American Psychoanalytic Association. Perhaps I would receive the inside scoop on the then most prominent aspect of psychiatry? Yes, I did as you will see. It wasn't pretty.

📝 Doctor's Notes

Lured by the coincidental appearance of a very attractive person, I trotted about on the ninth floor of the dormitory and found a portal to the personal world of psychoanalysis, where I met some of the people behind the analytic promise of psychological improvement.

Principle

Once again, I knocked on a door and a new adventure began. Try knocking on a few rationally/intuitively selected doors!

MY BUDDHIST CARTOON

In anticipation of my round-the-world trip, I applied for a visa to enter Nepal on the way to East Pakistan. In the New York City consulate visitor's packet was a rice paper square stating: "Good for one yak's nose cocktail at the Intercontinental Hotel in Kathmandu." I put the little treasure in with my passport. After stops in Los Angeles, Hawaii, Hong Kong, Bangkok, and Calcutta, I landed in Kathmandu with John, a Harvard graduate I had met in Bangkok. He was on a fellowship requiring him to stay out of the United States for a year and to write about it.

We rented motorcycles and headed for the Himalayan peaks surrounding the Kathmandu valley. We were stopped when the narrow road turned into stairs. We turned around and found the Intercontinental Hotel. The bartender had never before been presented with the rice paper square, but he treated us to a pair of cocktails and some food. The yak's nose cocktail was awful! That should have been a warning about what was to come.

Then we ate at the Blue Tibetan Restaurant where they served us water buffalo stew. A Nepalese man came to our table and unfurled his cloth bundle to show us some black gooey stuff to buy. We declined. (I later learned it was hashish.)

The next day we rode pedal bikes to the local Buddhist Stupa, a temple on a hill overlooking the valley. We entered the first-floor prayer room and were greeted by exquisite incense. Circular papier-mâché stalls hanging from the ceiling down to about three feet above the floor were placed at equal distances around the room. Within each stall, a single person could stand, light incense, and pray. Alone, together, praying. Cool! As we marveled at the serenity and feel of this place, a man in saffron robes came up to us and said, "The Lama will see you now." Wow, I thought, they knew we were coming! We are about to receive great wisdom! They are telepathic here!

With my heart beating fast, we were ushered into a second-floor room strewn with meditation rugs where other men in saffron robes were sitting. One man sat on a higher perch. Yes, he was the Lama. We stood in front of him, looking up. The silence lasted for a long time, it seemed. A beautiful, rich, full silence. Then, the Lama raised his hand and looked directly at me and said, "Do want to buy a rug?"

I was stunned.

I was in the highest mountain range in the world. Near the Buddhist Holy Land of Tibet before the Chinese took control. We were expected but not the way I thought we were.

Was I naive, even foolish to expect anything more from the Lama than a basic commercial interaction? Perhaps. But I had knocked on a mystic's door and discovered LSD, ancient teachings of the Kabbalah, the tarot, and astrology. I had knocked on the door of a Yale psychiatrist that led to the Good Friday experiment and unused data that formed the basis of my medical school thesis. I had knocked on a medical student dorm room door and was led to the daughter of a past president of the American Psychoanalytic Society.

Was I wrong to expect something magical in the mystical mountains of Nepal?

There are stacks of mountain guru cartoons. In one of them, the seeker, after a monumental climb, reaches the pinnacle and enters the presence of the guru who sits calmly, meditatively. The seeker believes he is about to receive wisdom. But the Holy Man then utters something surprisingly mundane like "the secret of life is to invest in low-cost mutual funds," or "If I knew the meaning of life, do you think I would still be sitting here?"

So that's what happened. I had entered a cartoon.

In the Himalaya Mountains, I climbed into a cartoon.

Riding down from the stupa, pondering the meaninglessness of life, I impulsively decided to ask Winnie back in New York to marry me. My worldview was shattered. Ontological shock. Seeking stability, I made a poor decision. Our marriage was soon annulled.

📝 Doctor's Notes

I stepped into a cartoon that shattered my belief in the lofty wisdom of gurus. This guru-rug wallah was first of all just a person trying to make his way through life. He had to earn cash like all leaders of organizations trying to keep the group afloat. "If you see the Buddha on the road, kill him." He's not really what you think or hope he is. Like the Wizard in *The Wizard of Oz*, he's a person pulling the magic strings. Our job is to learn to pull some of the strings ourselves.

Principle

When expecting synchronicities that present you with eternal wisdom, guidance, support, or contact with the Oneness, be careful. It could be the trickster at work, or maybe just a coincidence.

Also, this profoundly ironic step into a cartoon suggests that at another level or reality, our lives are being drawn by a clever cartoonist. Who might that be? You or . . .

That research trip to Los Angeles in the summer after my first year at Yale missed the target. I had wanted to go to San Francisco, not Los Angeles. Further tantalizing me was a series of articles in the *New York Herald Tribune* by Tom Wolfe. Gathered together, they became *The Electric Kool-Aid Acid Test*, chronicling the exploits of the Merry Pranksters led by Ken Kesey. The colors, the dancing, their psychedelically painted school bus, the gliding past cultural norms, and the characters in a real-life movie—something was happening there. I wanted to be there.

5

San Francisco

Another standard transition. Leave medical school and practice becoming a physician. Finally, I got to San Francisco.

ANDREW WEIL REDUX

At 7:00 one morning in July 1968, I stumbled into the cafeteria at Mount Zion Hospital in San Francisco to begin my medical internship. I sat down, dazed and confused. Someone tapped me on the shoulder, saying, "Hi! My name is Andy Weil. You are sitting in my seat." This was the same Andrew Weil who had written the 1963 article introducing me to LSD. He was a balding, round-faced guy with a big smile. Excusing myself, I piled some scrambled eggs on a plate and sat down somewhere else. Andy later nominated me for president of the intern class. Since no one else wanted the job, I took it.

The first rotation was on the neurology service. My partner on that rotation was the same Andy Weil. We followed two private practitioners around—one whose name was Roy Kokenge (pronounced "cocaine"). Andy had the most infectious laugh, sometimes triggered by Dr. Kokenge's name.

📝 Doctor's Notes

I think there were twelve interns. If we were all paired, then Andy could be assigned to one of the eleven other people, including me. So, the chances of Andy being paired with me was one out of eleven, or

9 percent, which makes the pairing only somewhat likely. The probability was lowered by the pairing taking place during the first rotation.

Subjectively, it felt like an even lower probability since I was glad to be paired with him. Statisticians do not include the subjective experience of the coincider in estimating the probability. I think they should.

Principle

Some random (statistically explainable) coincidences, like being assigned to the same rotation as Andy, can be remarkably fruitful. Their subjective meaning is a neglected part of the conventional probability estimate.

MUSIC OF THE SPHERES

Most of the time, being an intern was pretty boring. After 5:00 p.m. on those quiet winter evenings, released from the drudgery, I drove to the Pacific Ocean through gorgeous Golden Gate Park with its winding roads and magnificent trees. As they neared the ocean, the trees became increasingly bent by the relentless offshore winds. I would arrive at Land's End, where the ocean rumbled. Filled with joy and gratitude for the coast's quiet magnificence, I parked my trusty 1968 122S Volvo and strolled to the water's edge with a smile, preparing for the sunset. Sometimes the clouds became illuminated with magnificent colors— orange, yellow, red—and became the ceiling of a huge cathedral. I stood watching and listening to the lapping waves. Do you hear that? A vast organ is playing ecstatic chords. More chords. More chords. Was this what the ancients called the music of the spheres?

📝 Doctor's Notes

The ancient Greek Pythagoras guessed that the movement of the planets (the spheres) created sounds. Did he hear the same sounds I was hearing?

Modern science would claim I was experiencing synesthesia, the conversion of one sensory modality into another—in this instance,

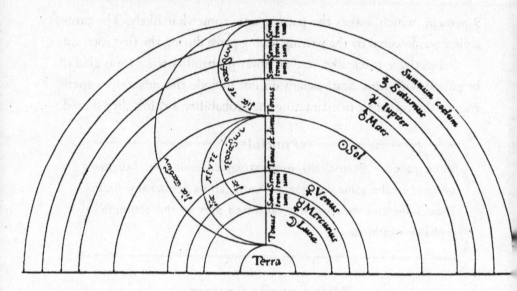

The Music of the Spheres

color into sound. For some people, sound can become color and shape. One of my patients created paintings by converting songs into colorful designs. Musicians loved her work. There are many other variations in synesthesia. I felt that I was listening to heavenly chords from the grandest of organs.

Principle

The natural world is singing to us. Try tuning in.

THE RETURN OF THE LIBRARY ANGEL

The time had come for me to apply for a psychiatric residency. I did not want to leave all the action in San Francisco. Having to work many hours had not allowed me to experience much of the hippie scene. So I applied to Stanford because it was close to the city and it had a good reputation. By the time I got to an interview, they had filled eight of their eleven slots.

My faculty interviewer was Fred Melges, a smart, warm man who examined me through the microscope of his thick glasses. "What books have you read lately?" he asked. I wondered if I should reply with the title of some boring Freudian volume. Instead, I said George Kelly's *A Theory of Personality*, the fascinating book I had encountered in the stacks of the Swarthmore library. Fred was startled. How could this intern know this book? To my great surprise, George Kelly's work was the basis of Fred's Stanford research. Kelly emphasized the future, not the past, in psychotherapy. We are *Homo prospectus*, often looking to the future, although psychotherapists spend an inordinate amount of time focusing on the past.

How did this coincidence come about? The internet did not exist in 1968. I did not know who would interview me. If I had known, I did not know how to look up the interviewer's research interests. Even if I had known that Fred was to interview me and it was a good idea to look up his research, I was too caught up in the San Francisco whirl to have gone to the medical library at University of California at San Francisco and searched through card catalogs.

Did I subconsciously see the book in Fred's bookcase? I am nearsighted and usually take off my glasses when talking with someone. My answer came from the clouds of intuitive knowing. I was accepted to Stanford and Fred volunteered to be my supervisor. His guidance provided the foundation of my first book, *The Structure of Individual Psychotherapy*.

📝 Doctor's Notes

Of the several faculty members interviewing prospective residents, how did Fred get assigned to me?

The George Kelly connection with Fred opened the door to my acceptance to the residency. My explanation: In my hour of need, I may have picked up the idea of Kelly from Fred's mind and the mental atmosphere of his office. Like a tuning fork being struck, my image of Kelly's book started vibrating to call my attention to it and to speak it. How I picked it out of the stacks at college is harder to explain. Perhaps it too resonated with some unformed ideas in my mind about the importance of the future in psychiatry. Perhaps I found it through a precognitive knowing that I would need Kelly for my medical school thesis and also meet Fred, the only psychiatrist on the Stanford faculty immersed in the work of George Kelly.

─────────────────── **Principle** ───────────────────

Our intuitions have access to immense stores of information in the psychosphere not readily available to our rational mind. I may have tuned in to the localized psychosphere of Fred's office—the ideas floating around his mind and reverberating off the walls. So listen to your still, small voice, to your heart, to your gut. Tune in and sharpen your understanding of their messages. Demanding situations can evoke unlikely solutions.

───

6
Psychedelic San Francisco

I WAS FINALLY FREE TO HIT THE STREETS of San Francisco. My first-year obligations at Stanford were minimal. I had to be in the outpatient clinic three days a week, seeing patients and attending a half-day set of seminars. On Wednesday evening or Thursday morning, my trusty Volvo and I headed north to the city. Ah, the glorious temperature change heading into the foggy city, especially going up Route 280. Passing San Francisco State University meant a 15 degree drop in temperature, time to roll up the windows and drink in the city with its promising adventures.

I spent the first three months of my second year of residency "doing research," which meant crashing (what we called sleeping) at the Yellow Submarine, a marijuana-dealing railroad apartment in San Francisco, and writing the foundation for my first psychotherapy book, a seventeen-year endeavor. During the second three months, I served with another resident on an inpatient psychiatric unit with maybe five patients to care for and a nursing staff that filled in for our incompetence. Then I spent six months on the heroin treatment ward at the Palo Alto Veteran's Hospital.

My two years of military service at the U.S. Public Health Hospital in San Francisco were followed by my final year as a resident. I worked half-time in San Jose and opened a little private practice in my house in the city.

That's the structure of those five post-internship years. Now the coincidence details.

THE WITCH IN GOLDEN GATE PARK

Near the beautiful Conservatory of Flowers on the east side of Golden Gate Park, she stood, wearing her colorful hippie dress, thumb out hitch-hiking. I had no obligation to anyone's schedule now. This was an ultra-free week between internship and residency. So why not? "There's a street fair in Berkeley," she said after settling into my Volvo's front seat.

Her name was Paula. She introduced me to the hippie subculture starting with helping me buy suede leather pants and a see-through gray ruffled shirt with a natural tan leather vest. At her apartment I used head-phones for the first time to listen to some of the great musicians of the late 1960s. Paula wanted me around her because I was a doctor, and she had broken her back. She thought the injury resulted from her doing black magic for money. She came from a wealthy family living near Palo Alto.

📝 Doctor's Notes

This portal to the hippie subculture opened because I took a chance on the unknown. Wondrous synchronicities followed. Paula opened the door to my becoming a part-time hippie during the first year of residency.

Principle

During any window of time in which the structure of daily life is loos-ened, you have the option of following suggestions from your honed intuition.

THE YELLOW SUBMARINE

Paula bought her grass, more recently known as weed, from Captain Bill, who lived in the Yellow Submarine. The first mate was his nine-teen-year-old girlfriend Liz, and his second mate was steward/grand-father-like Thaddeus Golas, who loved smoking unfiltered Camel cigarettes. He was writing his magnum opus, a very short book called *The Lazy Man's Guide to Enlightenment,* which became a hippie classic. Much of what he wrote came through his experiences with LSD. One day, Thaddeus made sure that I heard him say, "You are not needed for the world to change. It will change without you. You are lucky to be part of any group wanting to help make things better." That humbling clarity took years to settle into my ego.

For three weeks I lived with Captain Bill, Liz, and Thaddeus. Coincidences flowed through the Yellow Submarine, especially connections between the astrological sun signs of the grass customers and the current moon sign. If the moon was in Cancer, a person with the sun sign of Cancer came to buy grass.

Doctor's Notes

Moving through time in the Yellow Submarine, we were submerged in the magic streams of a new pop-up culture that was reviving ancient tribal thought patterns. The reality of astrology became more evident.

Principle

While many people travel to foreign countries like India and Peru to gather new information to bring back home, new cultures can be found within Western countries from which to learn about the interrelatedness of all things.

SMALL-TIME DOPE DEALING

Captain Bill had a kilo of dope to score. I wanted to experience the next level of the marijuana trade. Good profits were made because the stuff was illegal, so risk paid off in dollars. Bill decided to be clever. He set me up to take the fall if we were busted. My car, my satchel. We drove someplace. He scurried in and came out with a satchel full of grass. He looked around as in some low-budget crime movie, quickly got in the car, and said, "Drive."

Doctor's Notes

The number of illegal acts that go on without being caught must be very high.

─────────────────── **Principle** ───────────────────

Having no coincidence (like police coming around the corner as Bill came out of the house) can be more than pleasant.

───

OLD JEWISH LADIES LAUGHING

In the center of the gathering room of the Yellow Submarine stood a small square table a few inches off the floor with a heap of melted wax from months of melting candles. Surrounding the table on three sides were comfortable, colorful cushions for casual smoking, conversation, and financial transactions. The atmosphere was dense with floating cannabis, the mood was otherworldly, the music drifty and smooth. The conditions were ripe for boundaries to dissolve. A few times in that hazy daze, I thought I heard cackling laughter from what my mind's eye saw as a gaggle of old Jewish women. They were sitting around some kind of TV set with cheery eyes and big smiles of love and enjoyment watching me carouse at the Yellow Submarine.

Doctor's Notes

At the time I wondered about the reality of this audience of old Jewish women that I "saw." Now I've heard so many reports of contacts with deceased loved ones that I have begun to believe the deceased are hanging around you, me, and us. As I re-remembered those laughing women, one of them appears to be my grandmother, Omi. She thought I looked like her husband, my grandfather Bernhardt, whom I never met. She loved me and I loved her.

─────────────────── **Principle** ───────────────────

With evidence accumulating from mediums who can tell you things only you and your deceased loved one would know, to near-death experiences and evidence for reincarnation, perhaps you might consider, as I do, that our minds/souls survive the death of our bodies.

───

A Song for the City

Toward the end of each week of my first year, I headed back to the Haight. A serial coincidence happened as I entered the city on a section of the Bayshore Freeway. Back then the road into the city swung through a big curve. Elevated on that curve, as if on a roller coaster at an amusement park, I could look out over the crowded expanse, so colorful, so inviting, so ready for surfing the waves of city energy. Several times as I swung into that curve, a popular song of the time, "Crystal Blue Persuasion" came on my radio.[1]

📝 Doctor's Notes

I interpreted this song as saying, "Welcome to the City by the Bay."

Principle

Songs on the radio can demonstrate that our minds are more connected to our surroundings than Western cultures currently accept.

Synchronicity Spoken Here

Although the formal data have yet to be collected, coincidences and their accompanying mystical experiences increase with psychedelic use. During my Haight Street days, I had to keep telling myself: don't get blown out by all these coincidences. ("Blown out" was hippie talk meaning a swarm of amazing events crowding in can blow your mind.) Somewhere in the Haight, I saw a sign saying, "Synchronicity Spoken Here." It was just a fact of acid-hippie life to see lots of coincidences.

📝 Doctor's Notes

Patients undergoing psychedelic treatment for psychiatric disorders report an increase in synchronicities. I am pretty sure that some of those coincidences appear as aids to maintaining relief from distress.

1. Jmms429, "Tommy James & The Shondells—Crystal Blue Persuasion—969," YouTube website, September 29, 2010.

Principle

A culture that embraces synchronicities is also likely to find that coincidences can help with social as well as personal transformation.

THE SEXTUPLE AQUARIUS

A hippie chick turned me down in her bedroom in a house on Oak Street in the Haight-Ashbury district and pointed me to another room where I found an empty bed. A belt of Girl Scout merit badges was hanging on her wall. "Ah," I thought to myself, "a hippie chick with the need to accomplish." The next morning, we flirted at breakfast. We talked. Her name was Frances. We became involved. Great sex. Fun mind.

As I was about to write this section in early 2023, Frances emailed me to reconnect. We had not been in contact for decades. She described our encounter like this:

> *I came up to my bed, just a nest really*
> *And there was a beautiful man curled up in it*
> *With black curly hair*
> *With a small smile on his face.*
> *I wasn't sure he was asleep. I thought he was.*
> *Wandering the cosmos, he found me*
> *How does that happen?*
> *He made me laugh, so funny,*
> *So intensely beautiful.*
> *I loved being with him when he showed up*
> *Now and again.*

I remember the thick multisided lenses of her glasses perched on her nose. The shape of her face had sharp, crystal-like lines. In my tarot card deck, Aquarius, the Water Carrier, was symbolized by crystalline structures. Frances was born with her sun, moon, rising sign, Mercury, Venus, and Jupiter all in Aquarius. The deep crystalline lines of her appearance coincided with similar lines in the Aquarius card,[2] confirming evidence for astrological mirroring of life on Earth. In the card, shimmering water pours out of a large cup held by a young woman with a beautifully shaped body, much like Frances's.

📝 Doctor's Notes

Correlations like this one, between her appearance and the image on one of the tarot cards, were more evidence that there was something true about astrology and tarot. I enjoyed the synchronicity that she contacted me as I was writing our story for this book.

Principle

Take chances on chance and maybe you will chance upon some chancy situations and some beautiful coincidences. Take a chance on chance. As the timing of her contacting me indicates, we are interconnected in more ways that we realize. A possible explanation: my activation of the memory of our enjoyable times together reached through the psychosphere to her mind, prompting her to contact me. My imagining, remembering, and feeling our time together was a form of contact in itself. A telephone between minds.

THE PURPLE MOTORCYCLE JACKET

I had a purple leather motorcycle jacket that was given to me by an older woman who loved me because she liked the way I ran with the football. I reminded her of the father of her only child. But someone from the hippie house stole it. It had been on a bed on the fourth floor, but it had disappeared when I went to get it. A few weeks later, at a gas station, the thief and I crossed paths. That stunning purple jacket had few peers. He was wearing my jacket. I confronted him, did a little threatening, and got it back.

2. "Aquarius and the Star of Nuit," Tantrika Arts website.

📝 Doctor's Notes

This is very much an Internal GPS story. Somehow I got to the right place at the right time, which then necessitated action.

──────────── **Principle** ────────────

When you find yourself in the right place at the right time, you may need to seize the moment or the opportunity will drift away.

PURPLE SWEATER EYES

I went out to a dance hall across from Ocean Beach in San Francisco near the south side of Golden Gate Park. The crowd was murmuring at the back of the hall when the band started up and the female singer started pushing her tune to engage them. The crowd paid no attention to her as she strained for their attention. I walked out into the empty space between the crowd and the band, crossed my arms across the purple sweater my mother knitted for me, and stood there looking directly at her. She caught my eyes, her face lit up, energy flowed between us, radiating through me, reverberating through her. And then the action began. The crowd moved into the empty space and began dancing all around me. I had connected her to the audience.

I continued to stand there looking at her. During her second song, a guy came over and stood directly between the singer and me. He blocked my contact with her. The energy between the singer and me stopped. I turned around, danced a little, then left. By placing himself between us, he provided me with evidence of the brief energetic connection I had had with the singer.

📝 Doctor's Notes

What a pleasure it was to connect her with the audience! And then to have the connection further demonstrated by the guy standing in front of me to block the flow. Why did he need to do that?

Principle

A form of energy flows among and between people, especially on the dance floor. This energy can be amplified and diminished by our own actions. These energy movements may be less evident in nondance interactions. Awareness of interpersonal energy can be used positively and negatively. First you have to believe it exists!

PSYCHOTIC AT STANFORD?

Each week the first-year residents met with a faculty member to discuss clinical issues and sometimes to interview willing patients. With the group's permission, I invited Thaddeus Golas to talk about the enlightenment fueled by his LSD trips. They also let me invite Dickie the Astrologer to discuss the possible relationship between the planets, constellations, and human behavior. At another meeting, I did a tarot card reading.

Bob S., a kind and gentle fellow resident, invited me into his office to quietly tell me that I was psychotic and needed help. I had not yet discovered Carl Jung, who had formally researched astrology as an example of synchronicity. Instead, I told him, "I'm doing what your father does. Your father is a minister, and I'm trying to help people connect with the divine." Bob had nothing more to say.

Doctor's Notes

To this day, psychiatrists and other mental health professionals readily apply the "psychotic" label to people talking about synchronicity and meaningful coincidences. This ignorance remains a blemish on my professional colleagues. Yes, some people overwhelmed by their meaningful coincidences are psychotic, but most are not. Among most of those labeled psychotic, as I was, are those for whom the synchronicities become useful attempts to develop psychologically. We are normal people attempting to navigate difficult life circumstances. For others, a rush of synchronicities becomes a doorway to spiritual awakening. Perhaps psychotherapists will increasingly utilize coincidences to help people facilitate psychological, interpersonal, and spiritual change, as Jung did and I am doing.

I was an anthropological psychiatrist exploring the hippie intellectual-experiential world where synchronicities were common. Even the careful Sigmund Freud quietly considered parapsychological ideas.[3]

Hey, psychiatrists, listen to the patient! Some of these synchronicity episodes may be providing hints for psychological change. If you are bipolar and experiencing lots of coincidences, take a look at the life and work of psychologist Chris Mackey. His friends wanted him hospitalized for mania. In fact, he was producing the manic state on purpose to more efficiently handle a barrage of life challenges. In this rapid-thinking state of mind, synchronicities increased, many of which were helpful. As you can see from his book, *The Positive Psychology of Synchronicity*, he had it under good control and learned a lot.[4]

─────────────── **Principle** ───────────────

Meaningful coincidences often break the mold of dearly held conventional beliefs. Find ways to manage this ontological shock. If you are overwhelmed with synchronicities, you may need to find a coincidence counselor to help ground you. Talking with like-minded people is the best first step.

─────────────────────────────────────

YOUR PROBLEMS WALK INTO YOUR OFFICE

During my first year, John Beebe, a third-year resident, dropped a puzzle on me. Unlike Bob S. who thought I was psychotic, John was delving into Jungian concepts and was trying to use them. His quirky mind-twister—Your Problems Walk into Your Office—was directed at me as a beginning therapist. I was able to translate this comment into the idea that "Sometimes Your Patient's Problem Mirrors Your Own Problem."

This psychological mirroring also takes place outside of therapy.

─────────────────────

3. Janine de Peyer, "Uncanny Communication and the Porous Mind," *Psychoanalytic Dialogues* 26, no. 2 (2016): 156–74.
4. Chris Mackey, *The Positive Psychology of Synchronicity* (Watkins, 2019); Treacy, Sarah, "Synchronicity, Chris Mackey," Humans in Geelong website, May 31, 2020.

A few years ago, my good friend Amalia was having trouble deciding whether or not to meet somewhere, sometime. I was eager to see her. She said that she has trouble deciding things with other people because she can't tell if she is responding to what they want or what she wants. That was a good mirror of my mind as well. I too was having trouble distinguishing between pleasing the other person versus pleasing myself, and I sometimes don't know where to draw the line. Since that indirect lesson from Amalia, my boundaries on these situations have gotten clearer.

📝 Doctor's Notes

The personal meaning is clear: Take a look in the mirror that is the other person's mind to possibly reflect an external view of your mind. Events like this illuminate how we are connected with each other and how those connections sometimes manifest as mind mirrors.

Principle

Be open to the possibility that patterns in your mind may sometimes be mirrored by the minds of others. Be open to reflecting that mirror back on yourself. Help others to see that their minds are being mirrored in yours.

While a psychiatric resident at Stanford.

To the Victor Belongs the Coincidence

One of my psychotherapy supervisors at Stanford invited me to his home. I felt strange as he drew a square with names at each corner: WR, VR, WM, and BB. Huh? It was a puzzle for me to unravel. I tried. I couldn't. BB was me. WR was Winnie Rosen, my ex-wife; VR was her father, Victor Rosen, a prominent psychoanalyst. WM was Warren Miller, my supervisor. The answer turned out to be that Warren had been a patient of Winnie's father! At the time the puzzle was presented to me, Victor was in New York City, and we were at Stanford. I had become connected to Victor through Winnie; Warren became connected with Victor by being his psychoanalytic patient in New York, and I was connected to Warren through a random supervisor assignment.

Doctor's Notes

This coincidence meant to me that I was still connected to Winnie even though our marriage had been annulled.

--- **Principle** ---

Intense emotional connections seem to linger, as is sometimes reflected by synchronicities.

Three Thousand Miles Away and Twelve Years Later

The first sentence of the *Wilmington News Journal* (Delaware) read: "Strange things have happened, but here's one that ranks near the top. Two of Delaware's outstanding football players, rivals in high school 12 years ago, surprisingly meet for a pick-up touch football game 3,000 miles away in San Francisco. Neither had any knowledge the other was in the area."

Mike Brown and I were on opposite teams again. In high school we were running backs. In this game we each played wide receiver and had quarterbacks who could throw accurately. Our teams traded touchdowns. The game ended tied at twelve touchdowns each. Mike and I were the only scorers.

📝 Doctor's Notes

Mike had played in the Canadian professional football league and was a social worker in San Francisco. I was in the second year of my psychiatric residency at Stanford. How had we both ended up in the same city at the same time? And then had friends who invited each of us separately to play touch football the only time I played that game in my six years in San Francisco? I recognized him. I always admired his strength and speed. It makes a good story. Good enough for me to send the story to the Wilmington sports editor and for them to publish it. And it was great to see Mike again.

Principle

Meaningful coincidences illuminate the invisible currents that connect and unite us. Mike and I became fused during what was, for each of us, the biggest game of our senior year in high school. We were playing for the conference championship.

Who will you coincidentally reconnect with from your brief intense past relationships? These re-encounters suggest that we are part of an invisible web that creates bonds through emotional intensity. The implications of continuing connections like these are profound for our disconnected humanity.

FROM CRAZY ARTHUR TO THE BATS

In 1971, as the San Francisco hippie bubble was slowly deflating, Paula asked me to go to court to help represent her husband, Arthur, whom we called Crazy Arthur. He had a bracelet on his wrist that had the twelve signs of the zodiac on it. He would turn it every two hours to match the astrological sign that was on the horizon at that time (the rising sign). Crazy Arthur had been caught driving the wrong way on Oak Street off the panhandle of Golden Gate Park. The police had found some grass on him.

His lawyer, Mike Stepanian, was a rectangularly built man of Armenian descent with a big head and black curly hair. With Arthur between us, Mike and I strode up the long courtroom aisle to the judge.

The judge asked Arthur if he had anything to say. He did. Arthur brought out a roll of toilet paper and read from it, declaring, "Judge, I respect you and I respect porpoises." The judge interrupted him and declared, "Three months." As Stepanian and I walked out, he let me know he was from New York City, and that tomorrow, Saturday, he was going to play rugby in Santa Barbara. I said that I had played rugby for Yale, that we had played seven on a side against Columbia University on an island off Manhattan, and that I was better than the Columbia wing. He said, "Meet us at the San Francisco airport tomorrow at 8:00 a.m." I did and ended up playing rugby for the Bay Area Touring Side (BATS) for the next four years.

Commenting on the way I ran with the ball, one of the guys said, "He runs like a crab." My rising sign is Cancer, the crab. The rising sign relates to outward appearances, another confirmation that there was something to astrology, the forerunner of astronomy.

📝 Doctor's Notes

The hippie life was fading from San Francisco. Speed (methamphetamine) and then heroin were replacing the lighter drugs of grass and psychedelics. A lot of the tribe went north to Mendocino, Humboldt County, and beyond. I needed something else, and there it was—back to rugby. Right place, right time. Internal GPS plus seizing the opportunity by accurate self-promotion. I could run with the ball again!

------ **Principle** ------

One door closes and another door opens. Be sure to consider walking through the next door.

TOO COINCIDENTAL TO BE A COINCIDENCE

In 1972, the leaders of the BATS organized a six-week European rugby tour through Romania, Paris, London, and Wales. Six weeks! I never could do that. I was working full-time at the U.S. Public Health Hospital fulfilling a military obligation. I received a call from one of the guys going on the tour. "Hey, Bernie, come on along, make the trip." I said, no, I can't. A few days later another teammate called, urging me to go. How nice. Two different calls, what a lovely coincidence! So I asked the head of the hospital if I could go. He said okay! I don't know why.

On the trip, they explained the coincidence so it was no longer a coincidence. My teammates had conspired to give me the impression of independent action. But they had double-teamed me. Their invitation was no coincidence. Like the three girls showing up at my house in eighth grade—they had arranged it together. Another synchronicity is explained.

📝 Doctor's Notes

The illusion of meaningful coincidence was enough to flip me into asking the hospital administrator. What a trip it was!

Principle

If a cause for a coincidence can be identified, the surprising intersection of events is no longer a coincidence. This is why some people claim that there are no coincidences. They believe either that God/Universe/Source causes them or that they can be fully explained by randomness.[5]

So what looks like a synchronicity may have a human cause.

BERNIE, BERNIE

Our rugby team landed in Bucharest, Romania; we were the first American rugby team to play there. Our first team lost, and my team, the second team, also lost. We thought the ref called the games so the home team would win. The Romanian government could not tolerate allowing those freedom-loving Americans to win. Then we headed to Timisoara in the Carpathian Mountains, near where the mythical Dracula lived, to play our next games. I was glad to get out of dismal

---

5. Bernard Beitman, "What Causes Meaningful Coincidences?," Psychology Today website, June 8, 2022.

Romania where their secret service followed us around, working for the horrible dictator Nicolae Ceaușescu. We got a sense of the painful living experienced by those in repressive societies.

We took a train to Belgrade and then to the walled city of Dubrovnik on the Adriatic. That's where I met Rose from the United States who invited me to sleep with her. At around 6:00 a.m., we were awakened by a call echoing through those medieval streets: *Bernie, Bernie . . .* Pack fast and run! I had almost missed the bus to the airport.

On to Paris and then London for some more matches. In Wales the second team played on a rocky hilltop. We did not want to hit that ground. Aside from the rocks, all I remember is losing once again, while the Welsh fans kept chanting, *Bernie, Bernie, Bernie!* They seemed to like the way I ran with the ball.

Doctor's Notes

Two European countries and a similar chant for very different reasons. Clearly, I am the responsible agent. The chants helped memorialize for me this fantastic European tour.

Principle

Coincidences can serve as markers for special memories.

THE STRETCH LIMOUSINE

One afternoon I was sitting on the curb at the corner of Haight and Ashbury. I rolled a cigarette from a pouch of Kite menthol tobacco. As I felt the cool hot smoke tingle in my throat and lungs, a stretch limousine pulled up. Inside was Brian Rohan, the lawyer for Bill Graham, the impresario of the Fillmore and other psychedelic dance houses. Brian, who was also the apartment mate of lawyer-rugby player Mike Stepanian, said, "Hey Bernie, let's go for a ride." We cruised the city up into San Francisco's Twin Peaks as we talked a little and looked out the windows. After a while, we stopped at the corner of Haight and Ashbury, and I got out.

📝 Doctor's Notes

That was it. A coincidental, circular ride, back to where I started. The circle game.

Principle

You may journey far and wide only to return to where you started.

PARALLEL LIVES

Out in San Raphael, north of the city, a small-time grass dealer and his girlfriend lived with Deirdre LaPorte, one of the four female singers in Stoneground, a local San Francisco band. Like the other singers in the band, Deirdre wore 1940s long dresses on stage. She was tall with a dramatic presence. For one week, she and I started edging toward the romantic. One evening her band was opening for a big-name group (Crosby, Nash & Young with no Stills) at Winterland. I was backstage absorbing Stone Ground's performance. As she exited stage left, I touched her. She was electric. Electric Deirdre! More evidence of human energy fields. And then our thing ended. I composed a song about her cocaine use and sang it to her. She was not happy. A *hasta la vista* moment. Ah, the ephemeral nature of romance.

A few weeks later, I drove to the coastal town of Mendocino. Fog swept through the small downtown and the scattering of small houses. The moisture dampened the calls of seagulls. The rumble of the ocean created a mini–San Francisco by the sea. As I curled up in my sleeping bag on the cliff overlooking the ocean, the waves below lulled me to sleep.

On recommendation from someone who knew my interest in tarot cards, I knocked on the door of one of those small houses. Opening the door was a Deirdre look-alike in height and also wearing a '40s dress. Startled by the resemblance, I engaged her in a tarot discussion and left with a whiff of parallel lives in different locations.

📝 Doctor's Notes

The similarity was in height and dress. Deirdre and this person were different in many ways. I was struck by finding someone so similar in appearance to the person with whom I had a small bud of romance.

——————— **Principle** ———————

Each of us may have someone strikingly similar to us somewhere in the world. Doppelgangers ("double-goers" from the German) are two strangers who share a remarkable number of characteristics; most commonly they look like identical twins. Fiction contains characters who are eerie mirror images of each other, such as in Charles Dickens's *A Tale of Two Cities*. The probability of a match depends on the characteristics you select.[6] People may lead similar lives based on the complex interplay of cultural, social, and psychological factors that shape human experiences.

"HEY, DOC!"

As I came out of my San Francisco Victorian house on Hayes Street across from Alamo Park, I heard someone yell from across the street: "Hey, Doc, I want to talk with you!" How did he know I was a doctor? I didn't know him. Because my car was parked right next to where he was standing, I started talking with him. The night had begun. It was dark. He said, "I need some money. I'm in bad shape. Gotta have some money. How 'bout giving me some?" Standing near him, I said nothing. He became more agitated, reached into his pocket and said, "I need some *hairwine* (heroin). Give me some money. I've got a gun in my pocket."

As a fear-filled shudder passed through me, I asked, "Do you know Jack Reed at Reality House West (a heroin treatment program)?"

"Yeah," he said.

————————————

6. Zaria Gorvett, "You Are Surprisingly Likely to Have a Living Doppelganger," BBC Future website, July 13, 2016.

"You need to go see him. Do you have a cigarette?" He gave me one.

I got into the car as he was standing by my open window. "Can you give me a light?" He fired up a match and lit the cigarette for me. I drove off—relieved.

I was the psychiatric consultant at Reality House West where Jack Reed was the director.

📝 Doctor's Notes

Because I knew Jack Reed, I could fend off the threat. How he knew I was a doctor is hard to explain. If he had seen me at the treatment program, he likely would have told me. But that is my best guess. And even if he had seen me there, how could he see me clearly enough across the street? It was dark outside. Maybe he just called people doc.

Principle

In the midst of a threat, remain calm, listen to your intuition and maybe a coincidence will ride to the rescue.

SIMULTANEOUS CHOKING

It was around 11:00 p.m. on February 26, 1973. I was standing by the sink in the old Victorian house in San Francisco where I was living, age thirty-one. Suddenly, I found myself bent over the kitchen sink, choking uncontrollably. Something seemed to be caught in my throat. I couldn't cough it up. I hadn't eaten anything. I didn't know what was in my throat. I'd never choked for this long before. Finally, after fifteen minutes or so, I could swallow and breathe normally.

The next day, my birthday, my brother called to tell me that our father had died in Wilmington, Delaware, at 2:00 a.m. Eastern time. He was 3,000 miles and three time zones away; 2:00 a.m. in Wilmington was 11:00 p.m. in California. My father had bled into his throat and choked on his own blood at about the same time I was choking uncontrollably.

Karl Beitman and Bernie on the streets of San Francisco.

Doctor's Notes

The message to me was to remember my loving connection with my father, Karl Beitman, and to get seriously curious about how this coincidence might have happened.

First I needed to confirm that I was not the only human being who had experienced the distress of a loved one at a distance. The original meaning of telepathy was feeling, or *pathy*, at a distance, *tele*. Since the late 1800s, Western minds have known that we can feel the pain of others who are at a distance from us—telepathy. More recently it's called telesomatic. Indigenous people also know this experience. My subsequent research confirmed that many other people in the United States report this coincidence type, which I have named simulpathity, *simul* "at the same time," *pathy* "feeling."

———————— Principle ————————

We can feel the distress of a loved one at a distance. You have to believe it is possible. Experiencing one dramatic instance can solidify the belief.

SEEING THE FUTURE

It is sometime between 1972 and 1974. I'm sitting in the big orange chair retrieved from the MGM sale of its studio, sound stage, and movie sets. I'm dreaming of the future of my psychotherapy book, at the time in its third unpublished iteration. George Kelly's seminal book that guided my Yale thesis on psilocybin and opened the door for my residency at Stanford had been published by W. W. Norton. Another book that was highly influential to me, *The Psychiatric Interview* by Harry Stack Sullivan, was also published by W. W. Norton. I wanted my book to be published by W. W. Norton.

My second psychotherapy book, *Learning Psychotherapy,* was published by W. W. Norton in 1999. Dreams do come true.

🗒 Doctor's Notes

Imagining the future, creating the future, seeing the future? How do you explain my musings coming true? Teleological causation suggests the future causes the present by drawing us to it. There is a purpose or goal in nature, and things in the world strive toward that goal. This view is often associated with Aristotle's concept of "final causality," where the end or purpose of something explains the cause of its existence. In this view, I was drawn to a future with W. W. Norton.

Perhaps by energizing W. W. Norton in my mind, the seed for a future connection was planted by my personal agency.

———————— Principle ————————

Imagining helps to create the future. Make sure that what you imagine is what you really want, and that it is possible. Living in an igloo in

Nome, Alaska, and imagining a man on a camel coming to sell you a rug is highly unlikely.

ASSIGNED SEATS

It was 1974, my last year as a psychiatrist in training, and I had no place to go. Maybe Santa Cruz, by the ocean, to continue writing the psychotherapy book I had started as a first-year resident. In January 1974, eleven months after the experience of simultaneous choking with my father, I attended a ceremony unveiling my father's tombstone at his grave in Wilmington.

I delayed my return flight to San Francisco by one day because Bob Warner, my best friend from high school, needed help. He was about to be sentenced for burning down an ROTC building in Hawaii to protest the Vietnam War. In Philadelphia, which is near Wilmington, we discussed the details he needed in the letter I would write for him

The flight from Philadelphia to San Francisco required a plane change in Dallas. My seat would be assigned in Dallas. Sitting in the window seat was an attractive young woman with a very big watch. She looked over at me and asked for the time. She told me later that she thought I was a waiter. She then learned the truth. I did a tarot card reading for her and gave her my phone number. She was not going to call until she broke up with her current boyfriend.

In June, after many weekends together, we packed up our cars, hitched a trailer to my Volvo, and drove to Seattle, where she was to earn a master's degree in educational psychology. We were married four years later and have two sons.

Her name is Paula.

📝 Doctor's Notes

I like to think that my deceased father had something to do with arranging this marriage made in heaven, or at least far above the Earth's surface. Like me and my father and his father, we firstborn males were culturally obligated to have first sons who practice Judaism. And so it is. I am the fifth in the line as far as I know. My son Aaron is sixth. His son Max is the seventh first son and will celebrate his bar mitzvah. Will grandson Max follow in this patrilineal tradition?

Principle

The deceased sometimes seem to intervene in our lives.

LEAVING PARALLELS ENTERING

I entered San Francisco with Winnie and left with Paula. They resembled each other. Each was Jewish, about 5'7", brown hair, very pretty, and slender with wide hips. Their one-bedroom apartments were similar. Winnie wrote children's books. Paula was unpublished with her children's books. Each woman married me.

📝 Doctor's Notes

The entering and leaving partner parallels still have me shaking my head in wonder. Alpha and omega mirroring each other.

Principle

Sometimes we leave as we came.

SWINGING FROM VINE TO VINE

Life transitions open minds to coincidences. During the week between my internship at Mount Zion and residency at Stanford, I was freer than I had ever been. No school, no job, no parents, no marriage, no family. No place to be, no obligations. No one was tracking where I was. In that ultra-freedom, I had picked up the hippie Paula in Golden Gate Park. She linked me to Captain Bill, Liz, and Thaddeus, their Yellow Submarine, their grass and meditative womb in which I wrote the outline for my first psychotherapy book. Hippie Paula's husband, Crazy Arthur, linked me to Stepanian and rugby. Flying back to San Francisco from my father's tombstone unveiling, I found another Paula, future mother of my two sons. I was swinging from vine to vine like a happy monkey sailing between trees.

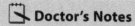 **Doctor's Notes**

This swinging from vine to vine characterizes many of my coincidences. Maybe they characterize many of yours.

---------------------------------- **Principle** ----------------------------------

To swing from vine to vine, you have to be looking for the next vine and be willing to believe there will be another vine there and then be ready to grab it.

7
How I Became a Tarot Card Reader

MOST MEANINGFUL COINCIDENCES take place in the unpredictable wilds of daily life. The mantic arts, like tarot cards and the I Ching, domesticate them by structuring randomness.

What will the future bring? What should I decide to do, this or that? The Oracle at Delphi was one source for ancient Greeks to find answers to these common human questions. At Delphi, the Oracle was a priestess to whom questions could be asked after she had entered an altered state of consciousness through which she communicated with the gods. Shamans throughout the world have functioned similarly, entering into an altered state to find, discover, and create futures.

The word *mantic* comes from the Greek *manteia* meaning "divination"—to be in touch with the gods or God. The mantic methods for prophecy use rituals with a wide variety of objects, including cartomancy (divination with cards), bibliomancy (opening a holy book), even cracks in the ground (geomancy), and shapes of animal livers (hepatomancy), as well as, yes, tea leaves in the bottom of a pot or cup. The I Ching is a form of bibliomancy. Throwing coins or yarrow sticks leads the seeker to one of 64 chapters in the I Ching. The mantic rituals rely on randomness to create a portal into the future.

My career as a tarot card reader began in Los Angeles in 1965 with that knock on Jean Brayton's door (described in the "New Haven" chapter). Several years later she sent me black-and-white pages of a set of tarot cards from the *Book of Thoth* written by Aleister Crowley. Thoth is the Egyptian name for Mercury and Hermes. Neither the book nor the cards were available in print in 1969–1970 while I was a medical intern. (There are many types of decks and new ones are published regularly. The Thoth deck has small variations from traditional decks like the Waite and Rider decks.[1])

I cut the seventy-eight cards out of the photocopied pages to make the deck and spent hours studying the symbols, looking for patterns in the twenty-two trumps of the major arcana, trying with each card to connect the title, the image, the Hebrew letter, the astrological sign, and the number. The image on each of the twenty-two trump cards represented an archetype: for example, Fool, Magician, High Priestess, Empress, Emperor, and Hierophant. The titles vary with different decks. These twenty-two individual puzzles strengthened my mental flexibility as I tried to apply the symbols to lived 3D reality.

The standard decks are based upon the Hebrew Kabbalah and further developed by Christians. Did they originate as a coded way to convey spiritual truths? Or were they developed to create a more complex game than the playing card deck of fifty-two, which had been invented earlier?[2] Did the ambiguity of the multiple symbols then allow mystically prone people to make up stories about them? The origin of tarot cards remains shrouded in mystery. Regardless of how they were developed, the cards sometimes mirror the mind of the seeker.

I memorized the card meanings and found a simple method for laying the cards out in a way that represented the past, present, and future of the person for whom the reading would be done. I made a simple leather pouch in which to fit the cards and tucked the overhanging top of the pouch into my belt and became a tarot card reader. Have cards, will predict.

---

1. "Universal Waite Deck," Tarot website.
2. Will Roya, "Debunking Common Myths about Playing Cards—& China," Playing Card Decks website, February 26, 2019.

Many of the people for whom I did readings were surprised by the accuracy of the past and present readings. They were often startled by the future predictions. The prophetic capacity of the cards lured me into wondering how they worked. Perhaps they simply allowed me to intuitively tune into the mind of the other person. Or was there something else to it?

In doing a reading we sat across from each other. I shuffled the cards and then asked the person to cut the cards into three equal piles and then put the deck back together. I went into a mild trance while opening the cards and read them like a story. I began to imagine a flow of information moving between and through the seeker and me, a river of time carrying unseen ideas. Shuffling and displaying the cards seemed like throwing the cards into this flow. I imagined that the thrown cards then froze so that their arrangement mirrored the moment of the flow for this person.

A new hippie chick showed up at the Oak Street house, interested in having a tarot card reading. I was attracted to her and predicted with the cards that we would hook-up. She led me to her temporary sleeping area, the basement of an abandoned house about a mile away. In the morning she was gone, leaving me sad, alone, a little used, and infected with the crabs (pubic lice). The message for me was: do not use the cards for personal satisfaction or gain.

Years later I found these words in Jung's introduction to Wilhelm's translation of the I Ching: "Whatever happens in a given moment possesses inevitably the quality peculiar to that moment." The I Ching ritual requires the seeker to ask a question and then throw coins or yarrow sticks to determine which of sixty-four hexagrams fits this moment and its question. Jung used the I Ching regularly because he found that the hexagrams often accurately mirrored his current psychological state. Here he had found ancient Chinese support for his growing interest in meaningful coincidences, particularly those consisting of mental events being reflected in the person's life.[3]

---

3. Carl Gustav Jung, Foreword to *The I Ching or Book of Changes*, trans. Richard Wilhelm and Cary F. Baynes (Routledge, 1968).

Tarot is based on the number 10, while the I Ching is based on duality—yin and yang. Tarot cards and I Ching hexagrams appear to be different symbolic manifestations of the same archetypical ideas.

According to my formal education, correspondences like these were to be ignored. There was no scientific support for such rubbish. Yet, before my eyes, as well as from the reports I received from others, there appear to be remarkable correspondences between the cards and events in 3D reality. I was taught to be open minded and to collect evidence. The evidence suggests that such correspondences are not uncommon. Perhaps the cards would help me explain some types of coincidences by recognizing the flow in which we are all immersed, like tadpoles in a creek. The cards lift us out of the current, creating a frog-like consciousness from which to observe the flow. The shuffled and spread cards mirror the flowing moment. A very important reason to study the cards and meaningful coincidences is that each, in a different way, provides glimpses of the reality in which we are mysteriously immersed.

8
Seattle

WHEN PAULA AND I MOVED IN 1974, I left behind my loosely structured single's life in the Bay Area for the more structured partner life in Seattle. Paula was earning her master's degree in educational psychology. I worked on my book. Structure dampens coincidence opportunities and maybe, sometimes, that's a good thing. It was for me. We spent many wonderful weekends riding bikes, hiking in the mountains, or strolling through one of Seattle's many beautiful parks.

BOREDOM

But writing most of the day in the damp, cold basement at 6208 41st Ave NE was boring. The Psychiatry Department of the University of Washington was a fifteen-minute bike ride from the house. So, I thought, why not pedal over to meet the psychiatry chair to see if there are any job openings? Carl Eisdorfer, a warm, smiley man, announced that he had five jobs open. "Take a look and choose," he said. The greatest need seemed to be for the head of the inpatient unit at Harborview Mental Health Center. I signed up for half-time because I was dedicated to writing my psychotherapy book.

📝 Doctor's Notes

Seattle at that time was in an economic slump. Boeing, the city's major employer, was doing poorly. People were leaving town. A 1972 billboard near the Seattle-Tacoma airport pleaded, "Will the last person leaving Seattle, please turn out the lights."[1] We didn't know this situation when we moved there. Paula was going to graduate school and I went along with her. That was it. They needed psychiatrists at the University of Washington and that became one of those coincidences that feels really good because of the result. I didn't know at the time that the objective probability of easily getting a job there was pretty high. The subjective probability felt much lower. I needed the job. And then, again, I was used to swinging from vine to vine, from level to level in this simulation-like reality called life on Earth.

A second woman named Paula had now guided me into a good situation. The first was Paula who introduced me to San Francisco hippiedom. My father's German girlfriend was also named Paula. He mentioned her name often.

Principle

In addition to synchronicities, some guides for you will appear as human beings in addition to synchronicities. Discern which ones to follow and which ones to let go. Keep learning which doors to knock on and then go strum your knuckles on that door.

INTUITIVE GUIDANCE

In the spring of 1977, after almost three years, Carl beckoned me to his office: "Either you go full time, or you are out." I couldn't do it, committed as I was to finishing my book. He shuffled me out of his office over to the vice chair who soothed my wounded ego. And that was that. I was crying.

In July, academic medical departments began their regrowth with new faculty and new trainees. I was also going to be without a job when July came around. Shortly before the July turnover, a gentle

---

1. Greg Lange, "Billboard Reading 'Will the Last Person Leaving SEATTLE—Turn Out the Lights' Appears Near Sea-Tac International Airport on April 16, 1971," History Link website, June 8, 1999.

inner voice advised me to make an appointment to thank Carl for the opportunity to be on the faculty. Warm and smiling once again, he reported that they needed a person to work two days a week on the consultation service. The psychiatric consultation service responds to requests for psychiatric evaluations of patients on medical and surgical inpatient units.

My lovely intuition again spoke up: "I will do it one day a week, not two, and I want to be half-time in the outpatient clinic." Carl agreed. He released me from the inpatient service at Harborview, doubled the half-time salary of $16,000 per year to full time salary of $32,000 per year for doing an additional half day on the consultation service. He set me up in the friendly confines of the outpatient clinic. This arrangement gave me the freedom to write, extra money to invest for the future, and provided more psychotherapy experiences.

📝 Doctor's Notes

Inner GPS? Right place, right time? I didn't know the department needed extra help again. But my inner knowing knew something. You could say that it was wishful thinking come true. But I didn't go expecting a reinstatement at twice the salary. I was going to express heartfelt appreciation for the opportunity to have been part of the department. Unlike wishful thinking, my body felt something genuinely real, believable, and necessary. It wasn't just a thought. It was knowing something that you don't know how you know. And knowing that you know. I had a voice like that speaking to me while I was running ninety-seven yards for a touchdown at Swarthmore. It said, turn left here, as easily as you read this sentence. We have capacities that are ridiculed by conventional scientific thinkers. Hearing voices does not mean you are crazy. Listening to inner guidance can be quite the opposite—helping to better manage living your life.

A bit of my personal trickster also played a role in meeting with Carl. I had nothing to lose and going to thank him for firing me was doing the opposite of the standard response of slinking away into the gathering dusk. Stepanian, the rugby player in San Francisco, called it "a double reverse twist."

Principle

Hone your ability to recognize, listen to, and feel your inner messaging. These messages may come as a still, small voice, or an urge from your heart, or a gut feeling from the intricate nervous system of your intestines. Some of the messages from your inner messaging service may be wrong for the current circumstances. Learn to discriminate the useful ones from neutral ones and especially those leading to negative outcomes. One source of problems for most of us is "negative self-talk"—judgmental criticism of what we are doing. Occasionally, that negative self-talk may prove to be a useful course correction for you. Again, learn to discern your inner guides. Learn to discern!

THE COINCIDENCE JOKER

I heard this joke: A guy keeps talking and talking about himself. The listener looks a little bored. The talker pauses. Seeing the bored look on the listener's face, he then says, "Hey, I've been talking a lot about myself. Time to stop. (Pause . . .) What do you think of me?" The conversation is still all about him.

A few weeks after I had heard the joke I was walking along the shore of Lake Washington with a psychotherapist friend. We stop. He looks at me and continues talking about himself. He's been talking about himself for quite a while. I feel boredom and irritation spreading through me. He seems to notice. He pauses. Then he says "I've been talking a lot about myself. What do you think of me?"

What? That joke again! This time in real life. I laughed inside of myself. Who's the joker here?

📝 Doctor's Notes

Like the incident with the Lama rug salesman, I was once again inside a cartoon.

──────────────── **Principle** ────────────────

There are lots of jokers in this Earth life. The best you can do is laugh and learn. Sometimes I think we are all in some kind of TV series as depicted in the movie *The Truman Show*. Like Truman, we need to discover that we are in this movie and figure out what to do about it and with it.

───────────────────────────────────

SERENDIPITY FOR CHEST PAIN AND PANIC DISORDER RESEARCH

Smart, friendly, and well-informed, Wayne Katon was consulting to the outpatient family practice clinic while I was consulting with the outpatient primary internal medicine clinic.

After a few years of doing that consulting, I was denied tenure at the University of Washington. The committee said, "Not enough data-based papers." I had twenty-five papers in the publish or perish game, but the rules had switched without my knowing it. "You need numbers!" They also claimed I did not earn enough money; apparently a few weeks per year on the inpatient unit was not enough for them even though I covered my salary. I think they objected to my working at home four half days per week. The acting dean with whom I played softball could do nothing. The vote was three in favor of promotion and eleven against. Pretty strongly negative. The faculty did not want me there. I was advised to resign. So I resigned.

Meaningful coincidences are more likely to happen during life stressors and transitions, but I did not know that then.

Standing in the hallway of the Psychiatry Department for the last time, I was deciding whether or not to say good-bye to Wayne. Politeness and respect urged me to do the right thing despite my misplaced feeling of competing with him. My knuckles rapping on his door once again became opportunity knocking.

On his desk was an academic paper on the relationship between chest pain and psychiatric disorders. The researchers had interviewed patients who had undergone cardiac catheterization and found that two-thirds of the patients with normal coronary arteries fit a psychiatric disorder, most likely some form of anxiety.[2] This finding meant that people with severe chest pain who didn't have heart disease had a good chance of having panic disorder. Wayne had sketched out a one-page research protocol to build on this research. I asked him for a copy. *The Ask is so important in our helping to create meaningful coincidences.*

Wayne's research culminated in the development, testing, and dissemination of "collaborative care," in which mental health specialists help primary care providers deliver effective psychiatric care, usually within the primary care setting. The collaborative care model focuses on medical patients with depression and other psychiatric disorders who would otherwise not seek mental health treatment. The Collaborative Care Model currently reaches millions of people around the world.

In my next job, in the department of psychiatry at the University of Missouri–Columbia, with Wayne's protocol in hand, and aided by several more coincidences, I did the required data-based research. As a result, I was promoted to full professor and became chair of psychiatry at University of Missouri–Columbia, a position I held for seventeen years.

📝 Doctor's Notes

This pushing yourself to do something you don't want to do can create right time, right place coincidences. Maybe it's the space between the "no" and the "yes" that opens it up. Or perhaps this is a form of Internal GPS. I felt it as an urge to do the right thing and say goodbye. However we end up explaining these happy accidents, they happen. And they can be life changers. But many don't happen unless you knock on the door or its equivalent and ask,

―――――――――― **Principle** ――――――――――

Look back at your life. Do you find any door knock coincidences? Serendipity has two forms—the weak and the strong versions.

―――――――

2. C. Bass and C. Wade, "Chest Pain with Normal Coronary Arteries: A Comparative Study of Psychiatric and Social Morbidity," *Psychological Medicine* 14, no. 1 (1984): 51–61.

The weak version involves looking for something and finding it an unexpected way. The strong version (the more difficult one to arrange) involves looking for something and unexpectedly finding something else that is very useful. I was intending to say goodbye to Wayne and found the key to a much better academic future than I would have in Seattle. And my wife Paula was very happy to get out of the rain. Embrace failure by keeping your eyes open for the next door to knock on.

9
Columbia

HOW DID I END UP IN COLUMBIA, MISSOURI? We had stayed in Seattle because of my work, but now it was Paula's turn. After two years in graduate school, she was ready to leave that drippy, rain-drenched, cloudy landscape. She was from Texas and needed the sun. We chose Columbia, Missouri, as a possible location because she had relatives in Kansas City, two hours west.

I applied to the Psychiatry Department at the university in Columbia and they accepted me, despite my having been asked to leave the Psychiatry Department at the University of Washington.

The tone of the stories in this chapter is muted compared to San Francisco. Context and geography strongly influence synchronicity and serendipity experiences. In this Missouri college town, I became a fully dedicated academic. I was working within the reigning materialistic paradigm that insists, without evidence, that the brain generates consciousness. The brain is necessary for us to be conscious here on Earth. It seems to act as a filtering agent for greater consciousness experiences. For a while, I became head of neurology as well as psychiatry, requiring me to think even more that mind is restricted to the brain. The materialistic paradigm generally excludes the potential benefits of meaningful coincidences because these experiences suggest that mind is part of our environment rather than entirely separate from it. We are not islands unto ourselves. There is purpose to our lives, meaning around us. All is not random. We are part of a greater whole.

The Katon coincidence appeared in my transition from Seattle to Columbia with my strong need to prove myself academically. Need and transition correlate with increases in coincidence experiences. After that major transition, which set the stage for future success, the coincidences tended to involve academic work. You can say it is all academic and skip this chapter. Or you can recognize that in the doldrums of restricted contexts, useful coincidences can reach your awareness. The results may not stimulate the joy, wonder, and amazement that accompanies coincidences happening in less structured, wilder situations. Several of these coincidences were very helpful for my academic career. They illustrate the value of synchronicity awareness in organizations and businesses, especially for leaders. Pragmatic as well as amazing.

ANOTHER DOOR OPENS

The chair and vice chair of the Psychiatry Department at the University of Missouri–Columbia knew of me from two of my articles published in their *Journal of Operational Psychiatry*. As I was applying, their limited budget suddenly opened up thanks to the departure of one of their faculty.

📝 Doctor's Notes

One door had closed, but another opened. I got a job in the place we wanted at the time we were ready to take it. Missouri turned out to have many more opportunities for me than Seattle would have, even if I had received tenure. Paula was much, much happier there.

Principle

In the face of disappointment or loss, keep your eyes open for new possibilities rather than letting your head drop in sadness. A drooping head is unlikely to see openings, possibilities, and opportunities.

A FRONT DOOR OPENS TO THE BACK DOOR

With Wayne's protocol to follow, I hit the ground running looking for chest pain and panic disorder research opportunities. Then this meaningful coincidence appeared: the back door of the cardiology clinic was directly across a narrow hallway from the back door of the psychiatry clinic. Geography is destiny! Cardiology outpatients could discretely step across the hall to the psychiatry clinic for diagnostic interviews about their panic disorder and depression, and fill out self-report surveys about anxiety, agoraphobia, and alcohol use.

With the help of three psychiatry-friendly cardiologists, each of whom wanted to have their name on more papers, I began several studies of cardiology patients who presented with chest pain and no evidence of heart disease. My psychiatry team interviewed more than one hundred outpatients from the cardiology clinic with atypical or non-anginal chest pain, which meant their type of pain suggested that they were unlikely to have heart disease. The team also interviewed ninety-four people with angiographically normal coronary arteries, one third of whom fit panic disorder criteria. In other words, upon visualization, their coronary arteries were not blocked enough to explain their chest pain.

One of the many conclusions from these studies was that if you were under forty and female, the chances were very low that the chest pain signified heart disease; it was much more likely to be panic disorder.

Two of the papers I published on the subject were collaborations with Wayne Katon. After the dust settled from all this research activity, I had authored or co-authored more than forty papers on the subject. As a result of all this data-based research, I was promoted to full professor with tenure. This successful path had begun with my urge to be polite and to knock on Wayne's office door.

📝 Doctor's Notes

When our department moved to a bigger outpatient space, this back door serendipity disappeared. Opportunity presents itself temporarily. As you have heard me say several times, take the opportunity when it presents itself. The flow of events can submerge a possibility and draw it away.

Principle

Jason Flom, CEO of Lava Records, created a term for not acting when an opportunity presents itself, as I mentioned earlier but
seems worthwhile to repeat. He called it a "non-moving violation."
This violation is the opposite of getting a ticket for a moving violation
while driving a car, like speeding or failing to stop at a stop sign. To
not grasp the opportunity violates your optimal path through life.
Grasping creates the coincidence.[1]

Geography is destiny. Where you live influences opportunity
potentials for work, healthcare, education, and romance. The internet has expanded possibilities for work and education as well as
romance. Yet for romance many people still use the old-fashioned
social group method. You meet, get to know, and learn from others
about real people in your geographical area. Seeing healthcare professionals in person tends to optimize outcomes. Serendipity still plays
a role by providing options, like the door across the hallway, that
require your decisive action to maximize your intentions and answer
your needs. Be alert, ask questions, imagine fulfilling your need, move
around, be willing to get lost, try new pathways. Remember that the
dog who trots about finds the bone, especially if that puppy is trotting near a butcher shop.

A diversified environment (either physical or digital) helps to
increase the likelihood of serendipity. The relative ease of traversing
an environment and its ability to catch your attention are also crucial.[2]

SWITCHING PLACES

For the chest pain and panic disorder project, we needed a psychology
grad student to collect the data, analyze it, and write it up. As part of
their graduate program at the university, each student selects from a

1. Bernard Beitman, "Coincidences and the Non-Moving Violation," Psychology Today
website, July 15, 2016.
2. Bernard Beitman (2022) Meaningful Coincidences. Inner Traditions: Rochester, VT
p. 52.

list of paid part-time research positions. We put in our bid. I found out after the assignments were made that someone who originally signed up for our project decided to switch to another. We got Matt Kushner, which was an excellent pairing for him as well as for us. Matt was really smart, very interested in studying anxiety, and a delight to work with. The original person would have done the minimum and gone on to something more relevant to their interests.

Doctor's Notes

I had cast my net out into the grad student pool without knowing what fish might take the bait. Two of them switched, much to the delight of all concerned.

Principle

Cast your net into uncertainty. You might find that what you are seeking is also seeking you. When the resulting match works out positively, we can only be grateful. Sometimes what appears to be a match made in heaven is a false promise. For a research project involving using AI bots to look for patterns in coincidence stories, I put out a wish for someone with AI credentials to complement my synchronicity knowledge and who wanted to do this project.

A person contacted me out of the blue wanting to do precisely what I had planned. Unfortunately, our personalities did not mesh, which meant this great coincidence would not lead to our collaboration. Coincidences are suggestions, not commands. Just because who you are seeking is seeking you, does not mean the partnership will work.

WALTER THROUGH THE PLAYGROUND

Matt and I became part of a multisite trial for a new medication for panic disorder and generalized anxiety disorder. These trials used the standard double-blind protocol—neither researcher or participant knew which they were getting, a placebo or the active drug. I wanted to know what influence readiness to change has on the outcomes for drug trials. Expectation influences experience as George Kelly and Fred Melges and my Yale thesis had taught me. Extensive research has demonstrated that readiness to change predicts outcomes for smoking cessation, treatments for drug addiction, and other behavioral interventions.

We found that readiness to change predicted outcomes for both the active drug and the placebo.[3] Most surprisingly people who were ready to change and took the placebo improved just as much as those who were not ready to change and received the active drug.

What?! The prevailing belief that the pills were responsible for the anxiety reduction was being challenged. And the drug being tested was similar to alprazolam (Xanax), which has definite effects on human brains. How could expectation so strongly influence outcome? My psychiatric colleagues did not want to believe it, just as more recently most do not want to accept the usefulness of synchronicity.

Our paper was turned down by some of America's finest psychiatric journals. The idea was even rejected for possible presentation at an annual meeting of the American Psychiatric Association. The slot I applied for accepted about 50 percent of the applications.

I then noticed a new journal called *Anxiety*. Usually, new journals are less stringent in their acceptances because they have not yet established themselves. One reviewer said "accept" and the other reviewer said "reject." When that happens, the editor decides.

Tom Uhde was the editor. We communicated about the paper. I asked him if he knew Walter Uhde who had lived across the playground from me in Wilmington, Delaware. We had been in the same grade in elementary school. When we were in junior high, Walter had accompanied me while I knocked on the door of a house with three lovely sisters. I needed support. Scary. I liked all three. It turns out that Walter was Tom's cousin.

I later asked Tom if my knowing Walter had had any influence on his decision to publish my paper. He did not remember.

---

3. Bernard D. Beitman, Niels C. Beck, William E. Deuser, Cameron S. Carter, Jonathan R., T. Davidson, and Richard J. Maddock, "Patient Stage of Change Predicts Outcome in a Panic Disorder Medication Trial," Anxiety 1, no. 2 (1994): 64–69.

📝 Doctor's Notes

I wanted to get that paper into a psychiatric journal. I'll never know how Walter Uhde being the cousin of the editor helped me. I like to think it did. The improbable coincidence was composed of two independent events: I knew Walter from our childhood and I met Tom because he was the editor of my last-chance-for-publication journal. Walter had supported me with going to see the lovely sisters. Tom now supported me by accepting my paradigm-challenging paper.

─────────── **Principle** ───────────

Weird coincidences happen. Their influence can sometimes be hard to judge. Did my connection with his cousin influence Tom's decision? Or was this just a coincidence, only a coincidence, a mere coincidence that would have had a positive outcome for me without Walter being in the picture?

─────────────────────────────

FLOATING THROUGH ANOTHER OPENING

In 1991, the Psychiatry Department chair retired. The dean asked me, a senior faculty, to become interim chair. I was thrilled.

The dean wanted the new chair to head both psychiatry and neurology. That was a one for two, a cheaper deal for him. None of the external psychiatry chair candidates wanted to try to bridge the two disciplines. Both psychiatry and neurology do focus on the brain, so why not?

The histories of psychiatry and neurology have diverged significantly. At the time I became interim chair, there were a few American departments of psychiatry and neurology still remaining. Most of those combinations had split into separate departments. Neurology was, and still is, very brain based with peripheral interest in the interface between psychiatric disorders and brain dysfunction. Behavioral neurology and neuropsychiatry overlap concerning problems such as Alzheimer's disease, Parkinson's disease, stroke, epilepsy, brain tumors, and traumatic brain injury. This slice of brain-behavioral disorders represents a narrow section of each discipline. In the mid-twentieth century, psychiatry was focused on the mind through the dominant paradigm of psychoanalysis. The chairs of many departments were psychoanalytically trained. Then came psychopharmacology, so the new chairs of those departments were focused on psychopharmacology and the brain. Then the fad of psychopharmacologist as chair faded away. It gave way to expecting new chairs to know business operations, to act like CEOs of corporations. Many combined brain-imaging research with their business skills. Today psychiatric research is deeply focused on brain dysfunction in major psychiatric disorders like depression, bipolar disorder, schizophrenia, and substance abuse. The foci are very different from neurology's clinical practice and research.

When none of the external candidates would take both psychiatry and neurology, I was again the only one left standing. Knowing this, a senior neurologist paraded into my office and confidentially warned me that if I took the job as chair of both departments, the neurologists would have "you holding your head in your hands." Nice challenge. So I took the job. After five years, the dean found someone else to be the division chair. I was much relieved.

📝 Doctor's Notes

Because none of the other psychiatry candidates would also take neurology, circumstances were arranged for me to take the job. Serendipity at work. Being head of neurology encouraged me to learn more about the brain. I could then write about the neurobiology of psychotherapy. But I was unable to think like neurologists, and they knew it. I remained head of only psychiatry for another ten years.

Principle

Sometimes getting what you want is a double-edged sword. In this polarized world, the good and the bad often ride together. Like many meaningful coincidences, this one started out to be very promising and ended with relief.

A TRIPLE DOUBLE

Hiring new people can be a chancy adventure. As head of psychiatry, I had to find and hire new faculty members. The usual process involved advertising in psychiatric newspapers and making phone calls to colleagues in other cities. My method was different. Most of the faculty I hired just showed up looking for work.

There were five women whose collective stories were particularly striking. Soon after accepting the position, each of the five became pregnant. The second, third, and fourth each had twins. The fifth had been trying to get pregnant for several years. She, too, got pregnant soon after being hired, but unlike most of the others, she didn't have twins.

The string of twins becomes yet more surprising, however. To follow a basketball analogy, when a player reaches double digits in points, assists, and rebounds in a single game, it is called a triple-double. My department scored a triple-double—three women with twins. The first woman, who had a single baby, stayed for a few years then took a job that paid twice as much in a warmer climate. Her departure represented a major loss to the department. The fifth woman joyfully raised her single child, but stayed with us for less than two years because her husband found a better job elsewhere. The families of the triple-double stayed. Each made outstanding contributions to the department.

📝 Doctor's Notes

When women of childbearing age find satisfying work, they become more relaxed and more able to conceive children, so having a new job can increase the likelihood of becoming pregnant. This serial coincidence in the "superfertile" environment of our department helped achieve the desired longevity of three excellent faculty members. People with reciprocal needs found each other. These women needed a safe, comfortable nest for their families, and our department needed helpful, committed faculty members.

How did it happen? Like many coincidences, several variables influenced their decisions, both personal and professional. Columbia, Missouri is an appealing place to raise a family. The vacuum created by our department's need and my calm belief that new people would turn up also helped to make this serial coincidence happen. (A serial coincidence involves a set of two or more events that are objective, that is, external to the mind of the person observing the events so that any other person can see the events. More commonly meaningful coincidences involve a private mental event that only the person experiencing the coincidence has access to.

Principle

Hurtling myself into positive uncertainty seems to have become a pattern being repeated in these coincidence stories. Like most people, you may be afraid of uncertainty, fearing the worst outcome and being grateful when it does not happen. Positive uncertainty may help to create positive outcomes because you are looking for options and opportunities instead of worrying and not looking around. For example, once during my football days, after a safety, the punter for the opposing team was standing on his twenty-yard line. The teams were ten yards apart in two lines, stretching across the field, looking at each other. I am standing back behind my team by myself ready to receive the punt. The coach had not designed a play for this situation. My job was to catch the ball and run forward into who knows what or where, while the eleven members of the other team try to bring me down. I had to be positive about the uncertainty to look for ways to gain good field position for my team.

What do you think about running into uncertainty? By recording and examining your coincidence stories, you may find some repeated patterns that have been obscured by the details and emotions. Being calm in the storm of uncertainty with clear intent and willingness to grasp possibilities seems to help bring about positive results.

A PAPER CHASE

Scoring a lead article in the *American Journal of Psychiatry* counts as a great accomplishment in academic psychiatry. I put one together about psychotherapy integration based on ideas developed in my book *The Structure of Individual Psychotherapy*, published in 1987.

After the paper was published, Chinese psychiatrists had to surreptitiously obtain papers like this paper. Chinese authorities prohibited reading many non-Chinese publications. Dongmei Yue, a young psychiatrist at China Medical University in Shenyang, was researching psychotherapy and, through a roundabout route, secured a copy of my article. That led to a delegation of Chinese faculty members that included Dongmei, the chair of her department, and their chief psychologist, visiting our department in Missouri. They then invited me and two colleagues to visit them in China for a ten-day circuit, with my giving talks on psychotherapy. In Shenyang and in Dalian, China, I looked out into the audiences while Dongmei translated what I said. I saw many almost familiar faces. Aside from the eyelid shapes, some looked like people I knew. It was startling.

My son Aaron, age twelve, came along. He played basketball with other teenagers. We rode bikes in the dark and made sure not to wander too far from safe people or places. Most people in Shenyang rode bicycles in 1994. Only the very rich had cars. The people on the streets stared at us, having seen so few Caucasians. China has since changed immensely.

At the goodbye ceremony, the president of China Medical University pleaded with me to take Dongmei back with us. Once we figured out a way to pay her, she was living in Columbia with her husband and helping me develop a training program in psychotherapy. Three years later we produced a training manual for beginning psychiatrists to learn the basics of psychotherapy. For our work, entitled *Learning Psychotherapy*, we received two national psychiatric awards.

📝 Doctor's Notes

A lead article in the leading psychiatric journal led to an award-winning psychotherapy training program. Each of us found someone we did not know we were seeking. The keys were my writing the article, her seeking and finding it, and then contacting me. I needed her to fulfill my vision of a psychotherapy training manual, and she wanted something from me. She became a child psychiatrist and eventually secured a very good position in San Francisco.

I love these mutually beneficial coincidences!

Principle

The repercussions of your actions may benefit others. How many of those impacts do we never learn about?

THE SOFTBALL DEAN

My mother thought that getting tenure meant that after ten years on the faculty, I would get a vacation. (Tenure sounds like ten years.) She was kind of right. Back in the old days, the newly tenured faculty member was often granted a sabbatical of six to twelve months—money and time to study with a renowned individual in a fascinating place. But not anymore.

As I mentioned in the Seattle chapter, after almost ten years on the faculty of the University of Washington, I was up for promotion based on the usual publish-or-perish paradigm. I had more than twenty-five papers published in peer-reviewed journals, which at that time seemed like enough. Nope. Not enough. They were not data based. Need numbers. I was asked to leave the ivory tower.

When I had been asked to leave the University of Washington, a friend in high places—David Dale—was there for me. As I mentioned earlier, he was the acting dean of the medical school when I was asked to leave, and we played softball together. I repeat what he told me: "The vote wasn't even close. Three votes in favor and eleven votes against. I can't help you."

Years later, David Dale, no longer the acting dean, dropped by my office at the University of Missouri–Columbia. He was receiving an Honor Society award there. With a smile of deep satisfaction, he congratulated me on becoming chair of the department of psychiatry. My new job confirmed his belief in my ability. The circle closed.

📝 Doctor's Notes

How did my softball-playing friend end up coming to the University of Missouri–Columbia for the Honor Society lecture? He really did want to help me get promoted at the University of Washington but could not. Our seeing each other felt good for me and closed a circle in his heart and mind about wanting my success and being able to see it. Being fired can turn out to be the best outcome. Seattle gave me a goodbye present to make that success possible. It was a very satisfying meaningful coincidence to have David Dale receive an award from the place I was working. I guess he had to get an award from someplace, and the roulette wheel of life had him show up in my office. Random or something else?

Principle

May you experience the loveliness of a closing synchronicity circle!

THE IMPROBABLE STATISTICIAN

In 2006 I began research into coincidences by asking a basic question—how common are they? The research was divided into two stages. First, collect the data. Second, analyze and write up the data and conclusions. Psychology graduate student Elif Celebi helped create the Weird Coincidence Survey and collected the data. The second step, the statistical analysis, required someone with good training in statistics and an interest in working with us. We received only one applicant, Stephanie Coleman. Smart and shy, she was perfect for the required intricacies. She said, "This study of coincidences makes me more interesting at parties." She was the right person at the right time.

She wrote two excellent papers on our findings, which helped her to get a good faculty position.

📝 Doctor's Notes

Successfully casting out for a needed someone seems to be another pattern of my coincidence life.

--- **Principle** ---

Once again, the importance of action in fulfilling a need is illustrated.

No Answer

As chair, I had financial discretion. I invited physicist Victor Mansfield to present about synchronicity, physics, and Buddhism. As we talked after his excellent presentation, he took me aside and asked, "I have an inoperable brain tumor. I will die soon. I have so much more work to do with synchronicity. Why am I being stopped like this?"

I had no answer.

In the village of Matlab, three rivers away from Dacca, East Pakistan (now Bangladesh), researchers were studying the transmission of cholera. I visited the village in 1967 as a medical student at the Cholera Research Lab in Dacca.[4]

The researchers discovered that the people of Matlab often became infected after they had been visited by someone from another village. The visitor, like everyone else, defecated in the pond directly across from the village itself. Villagers took their drinking water from the same pond on their side of the pond They did not know that cholera could spread throughout the pond contaminating the water they drank.

The Matlab cholera story resembles much of humanity now. Like the villagers of Matlab we keep putting pollutants into our atmosphere and into nature while ignoring the harm we are doing to ourselves by re-absorbing those contaminants

A schoolteacher in Matlab invited me to tea at the tea shack. He asked me, "The streets of America are paved with gold. Why I am here instead of there?"

I had no answer.

---

4. "Matlab (Bangladesh)," Wikipedia website.

📝 Doctor's Notes

The same question, two men I hardly knew, half the globe and four decades apart, asked "why me?" Who was I to them? An all-knowing human who had an answer to one of life's most perplexing questions? Weren't they implicitly asking for a way out of their own terrible dilemma? They were drowning in deep waters of uncertainty. They were pleading with me to throw them a life preserver. My efforts to increase the use of coincidence have become my partial answer to this question from others, including myself.

Principle

Meaningful coincidences can provide clues to how reality works, including existential questions like why we are here and what happens after the body dies.

After seventeen years of being chairman, I'd had enough bureaucracy. I had been "institutionalized" since age five with one free week between internship and residency. I would now go on to become a recovering academic.

10
Charlottesville

FREED FROM ACADEMIC STRUCTURES and now no longer living with Paula, I could more easily float on mind currents passing by and through me.

How did this move happen? With Paula's help, I was drawn to Charlottesville where the University of Virginia's Division of Perceptual Studies (DOPS) is located. It is the only academically housed parapsychology unit in the United States. DOPS is primarily interested in extraordinary human experiences, such as psi (telepathy, clairvoyance, precognition and psychokinesis)—near-death experiences, and reincarnation. With these researchers, I found support for my coincidence interests.

Within twenty-five minutes of Charlottesville are three spiritual organizations using scientific ideas to investigate the mysteries of our existence. Each supports itself by instructing seekers in their methods of spiritual unfolding. The Monroe Institute uses binaural beat technology to have people have out-of-body experiences and make contact with deceased loved ones. The Synchronicity Foundation used sounds to aid people to experience the vast oneness while meditating; their form of synchronicity involves synchronizing brain waves. The Synchronicity Foundation has now changed course with the death of its leader. Yogaville provides silent retreats following the teaching of Swami Satchidananda for yoga practices, meditation, and yogic philosophy. Three hours away in Virginia Beach is the Association for Research and Enlightenment (ARE) founded by the seer Edgar Cayce who went into trances through which he found solutions to people's medical and other problems. Along with DOPS, these organizations signal a vortex of spiritual activity in the area. Perhaps this Charlottesville vortex contributed to the coincidences I experience here.

Karlen and the Duck Boat

Before Paula and I separated, our family was on vacation in San Francisco. On this trip Aaron, age twenty-eight, wanted to go to City Lights bookstore, so we piled into our rental car and Karlen, age twenty-four, drove like a Russian taxi driver through the Broadway tunnel into North Beach. It was March 18, 2011, around 1:00 p.m. At the coffee shop, Karlen, who was getting a master's degree in urban planning at the University of Illinois–Chicago, was telling us about his

Sons Aaron and Karlen, St. Mary's Glacier, Colorado.

homework assignment—planning for commuter transportation along Lake Michigan in the year 2050. He was describing the use of duck boats, those amphibious vehicles that could transport people from port to port, and then, by dropping the duck boat wheels, transfer them to their cars or other ground transport. Duck boats are pretty sizeable vehicles. Once, a duck boat captain was distracted while texting on his cellphone and missed seeing a barge that hit the boat and led to the deaths of several passengers. As we discussed the distraction that led to this tragedy, Karlen leapt up from his seat and pointed to the window. "There's a duck boat out there! I'm going to get a picture." He came back, shaking his head. The boat, wheeling past the window, was quacking. We laughed.

📝 Doctor's Notes

Our family of four needed something to lighten up the mood. The parents' marriage was soon coming to an end.

Principle

Sometimes coincidences are to be enjoyed in the moment—funny, numinous (mystical), artistic, enthralling, inspiring, and worthy of a stand-up comedian.

TENNIS BASKET, ANYONE?

On June 7, 2014, I went to play tennis on the courts of Charlottesville High School. As I started warming up, a woman with two preteens started practicing two courts down. She shouted instructions and compliments to the boy while the girl hit off the backboard. After about ten minutes, Will, my tennis partner, drove up and called to me from outside the courts. He said he had a present for me as he lifted a tennis basket in the air—one of those metal cages for carrying lots of balls. I shouted back that I already had one. Just then the woman two courts down shouted that she needed one. She had planned on buying one today for her children. It was a perfect fit!

📝 Doctor's Notes

Without the woman hearing our shouted conversation, there would have been no meaningful coincidence. Again some form of action brings incidents together to create a coincidence.

Principle

I wonder how often reciprocal needs could be met if people gave voice to them. What you are seeking, may be seeking you.

JUNIOR ACHIEVEMENT

On August 6, 2020, Karlen and I were talking on the phone about setting up a business structure for The Coincidence Project, which I will describe later. I told him doing this planning was like Junior Achievement when I was in eleventh grade. Under the guidance of an experienced businessperson, our group had set up our own little company by making a product ourselves (tiled hot plate stands) and selling them. Karlen had never heard of Junior Achievement. A few minutes later, he got on the elevator of his apartment building and was greeted by a woman talking to another person about Junior Achievement.

📝 Doctor's Notes

Karlen likes to fight against the existence and value of synchronicity. I enjoy it when they appear directly in his face like this one.

Principle

Ideas seem to float around in a local psychosphere and are picked up by various open minds. Listen and you will also see or hear what you have recently been thinking or talking about from someone you don't know.

A PAST LIFE APPEARS AT DOPS?

The Division of Perceptual Science (DOPS) met every other Tuesday in seminars around the fascinating subjects the researchers were studying.

Sometimes the meetings were attended by a student at UVA. One of them introduced herself to me and suggested, as she had to others, that we meet up.

We met at a local coffee shop and instantly held hands for the hour or so we talked. My arms and shoulders melted into her arms and shoulders. We were for a time one upper body. Afterward, I went home to lie on the couch reverberating from the contact. Her name is Amalia.

Once, we were sitting together in the front seat of my car. She put her hand near my waist and then put it near her waist. "Same thing," she said, meaning the same energy. We are both Pisces, birthdays two days apart. Mine February 27. Hers, March 1. We blend. We blur. We dance.

Of course, ours was an unusual relationship, a seventy-five-year-old man driving to a college dormitory to pick up a student and go someplace together.

My feelings for her were unlike any ever before. My heart was a torrent of intense emotion pouring out from me to her. It was more than I could handle well. Our relationship taught me how two people can love each other deeply without having sex together. I became her spirit grandfather.

I thought I knew her from the past life I felt as a teenager when I may have committed suicide in a Nazi concentration camp because we could not be together.

📝 Doctor's Notes

While a friend told me I had found my twin flame, Amalia helped to correct that impression. She made it clear in her beautiful ways that I was her spiritual grandfather, not a romantic partner. She continues to emphasize the importance of intergenerational love and how our society over-emphasizes romantic love. Her hippie elder is very important to her. Over the many years we have known each other, we have been a significant help to each other. I helped her find a partner around her age. She has prepared me to be able to love someone closer to my age. She has helped me process problems with a mutual acquaintance.

─────────────── **Principle** ───────────────

As for twin flames, a Greek legend suggests that each of us was once one half of a whole until we were separated, and now we roam the world looking for our other half. It's a beautiful idea that seems to apply to some pairs. As in my case, circumstances may inhibit or prevent rejoining in the roles of the previous lives the two had together. The yearning to find love with a twin flame fueled the creation of a deceptive, cultlike organization called Twin Flames Universe.[1] Be careful about being too open to New Age promises.

TELEPATHY IN NATURE

I'd met Alice a few times while hiking the mountain at Mint Springs near Crozet, Virginia, twenty minutes west of Charlottesville. One day she was with a man whom she introduced to me as Adam. As we talked, the image of a high school friend came into the video screen in my mind. The name of my high school friend was Dave, but we often teased him by calling him George. I looked at Adam and confidently called him George. That turned out to be his real first name, which only a few people used with him. How had I known?

Doctor's Notes

Somewhere from his being, probably the biofield surrounding him, I picked up this fact and was confident enough to quietly blurt it out.

─────────────── **Principle** ───────────────

Telepathy that occurs in the same space probably has a different mechanism than telepathy at a distance. Local telepathy should have a different name since the *tele* in *telepathy* means "at a distance." Each of us has a bioenergetic field that contains informa-

─────────────────────

1. See Esme Mazzeo's article, "Where Are Twin Flames Universe Leaders Jeff and Shaleia Ayan Now?" on Business Insider website, November 8, 2023. The contemporary cult inspired twin docuseries on both Netflix and Amazon Prime Video.

tion. I think it is possible to intuitively read information in that field.

MY CAPTAIN, OH MY CAPTAIN

Some weeks later, I was hanging around on a large float in the lake at Mint Springs. A man climbed up on it with his two young sons. I said, "Hi Captain!" He replied, "How did you know I was a captain?"

Doctor's Notes

Another quick read, perhaps by the way he stood, his haircut, and more. I just knew. Telepathy adds to information about someone from generally unacknowledged nonverbal sources.

Principle

Another instance of local telepathy is illustrated here. Again, I suggest that there is energy and information in human biomagnetic fields (auras) that we can pick up under the right conditions. Being out in nature, away from the stimulations of homes, towns, and cities probably increases our capacity to pick up information from auras.

THE LAND HOLDS MEMORIES

While attending a dance workshop on Cortes Island, British Columbia, I stood on a little cliff overlooking a beach and some islands. I began chanting. The chanting took me over. I became the chanting. Never had I made beautiful sounds like that before or since. I seemed to have picked up the memory traces of the Indigenous people still on the beach below me; they often lived, fished, and hunted there.

Doctor's Notes

Tuning in to the energy-information held in a geographical space is a capacity that seems to be latent in human beings.

Principle

Geo-psychometry refers to this kind of experience. Being outside, being in natural surroundings, increases the likelihood of intuitive knowledge.

FILLING IN THE BLANK

In his studio, John D'earth, Charlottesville's dearly beloved jazz trumpeter, was talking to me about ideal human love. The conversation triggered a song memory in me. I start singing:

> *When somebody loves you*
> *It's no good unless he loves you all the way*
> *Through the good and lean years*
> *And all the in between years*
> *Come what may . . .*

John stopped my vocalizing, surprised. He said: "I have been making a list of songs that are about enduring love. Here's my list. I knew there was one I forgot. That's the one!"

Doctor's Notes

I felt great filling in John's blank by spontaneously singing the missing song.

Principle

You may receive an answer to a question without having to ask. Did I pick up the blank in John's information-energy field? Let yourself think that is possible.

MIRRORS

I bought some blue-framed glasses because I thought they were cool. I put them on with my back to the patient who had just walked in. When

I turned around to surprise her, she was wearing glasses for the first time in twenty or so sessions. She normally does not like to wear them, but felt the urge to do so before coming in.

The patient thinks in symbolic realism. There are many symbols in daily life that reflect back our minds, conflicts, and questions, and these symbols may be handled like dreams, novels, plays, and movies.

We laughed a lot. We spent some time discussing the meaning of this coincidence. Since she is a writer, I asked her to write an essay entitled "A Pair of Glasses." She laughed when I explained that this title is a condensation of the more accurate description: A Pair of a Pair of Glasses.

Laughing together strengthened our already close relationship. The mirrored glasses suggested that we were traveling on similar wavelengths. What does it mean as part of her therapy with me? How can we use this synchronicity for her development? What does it mean for me?

We concluded that it meant we were seeing eye to eye.

Doctor's Notes

It was another example that showed me and another person how our minds are connected with each other.

Principle

The movie *On Being John Malkovich* flourished its ending by putting John's head on all the people he interacted with.[2]

"You are me and I am you and we are us together," are the words from "I Wrote a Song" by Mae Muller.

The Beatles said it this way in the song "I Am the Walrus": "I am he, as you are he, as you are me, and we are all together."

Our environment, and those people in it, can mirror our minds perhaps because each mind operates within the same mental atmosphere, the psychosphere.

---

2. Focus Features, "Being John Malkovich | John Malkovich Goes into His Own Head," (minute 3:50–6:20), YouTube video, December 3, 2022.

11

I Become a Coincidence Author

THE PROCESS OF FINDING A PUBLISHER for a book intended for a general audience can be fraught with frustration. The only solution is to keep on keeping on, or as we learned to say on Haight Street, keep on truckin'.

MY EDITOR-TO-BE SHOWS UP AT DOPS

I'd never written a book for the general public. My three previous books were academic ones geared toward psychotherapists and psychotherapy trainees. This time I was pounding away on my keyboard, using words on a page to understand the ambiguous, complex territory of coincidences, synchronicity, and serendipity.

How to organize this first book? I thought maybe I should follow the pattern of the *New York Times* bestseller titled *There Are No Coincidences* by Robert Hopke. He had organized the stories in his book by ordinary life categories—romance, family, work, health, ideas, spirituality. Ok, if I did that, I could then just fill in the blanks.

But what about getting an agent? I had no track record. Sure, Andrew Weil connected me with his high-powered New York agent who gave me a good story to include in the book. But the agent wanted data from prospective studies. All I had was a valid and reliable survey. I walked into his Madison Avenue office pretending that maybe something could happen. It seemed so promising. But, no, it was not.

One day in 2009, I was presenting what I knew about coincidences at the Division of Perceptual Studies when in walked a new person at the meetings, Patrick Huyghe. He liked what he heard and asked me to write an article for *EdgeScience*, a magazine he was the editor of for the Society for Scientific Exploration. He then ended up editing my book *Connecting with Coincidence*, gave it this title, and after many uninterested literary agents, connected me to Lisa Hagen, whom he knew personally. Patrick and I have become good friends. Lisa placed the book with Health Communications.

📝 Doctor's Notes

Patrick walked in at just the right time to tune in to my synchronicity songs. He seized the opportunity for an article for his magazine, and I seized the opportunity for a connection to the publishing world. And we each found a new friend.

Principle
Timing! Be alert in times of need. What you are seeking may be somewhere in the vicinity.

A DOOR OPENS TO BLOGGING

The head of the student mental health clinic at the University of Virginia was leaving his job and needed an office for his private practice. Another friend from The Division of Perceptual Studies (DOPS), Frank Pasciuti, needed to fill the vacant office in his building. I put them together. The former head became one of Frank's office mates. The former head was blogging for the *Psychology Today* website. "Bernie," he says, "they like to have people with academic credentials doing blogs for them. Shall I introduce you?" And so, in 2016, I began my synchronicity postings at the popular magazine's website. Coincidentally (or was there a relationship) *Psychology Today* magazine soon afterward published an article by a psychiatrist insisting that all coincidences come from a random universe explainable primarily by probability and statistics. Friends of mine thought that maybe the editors at the magazine were countering my insistence on personal responsibility for coincidences as well as my suggesting some nontraditional scientific explanations. I had data to support the commonality of coincidences and their usefulness in psychotherapy. Despite the controversy and because of the more than 1 million views of my hundred-plus posts, the editors added an additional category to their list of psychology topics—synchronicity.

But recently my editor sent me this note in an email: "Just FYI there is no editor on staff who sees your content as a perfect fit here. I wonder if there is another platform that would work better for you." After more teetering on the edge, I realized the obvious—write about the *psychology* of synchronicity.

📝 Doctor's Notes

I connect a man needing an office with a good friend of mine, and I start writing a blog for *Psychology Today*, with some subsequent turbulence. So, my dear editor, what are you saying? Are nonrandom explanations not the perfect fit as preferred by mainstream science? To keep the string of posts going, I wrote a few posts that were shaped like articles in the *Psychology Today* magazine itself. With my understanding of psychotherapy, I now rely on my extensive knowledge of psychology in writing the blog posts. The editor is satisfied most of the time.

Principle

Try to find value in the restrictions imposed on you by the context in which you are working.

NOT YET READY FOR PRIME TIME

While walking in the woods one day, the question came to me, "Are you ready to be a little famous?" I said, a little tentatively, "Yes, I am." Soon afterward, psychologist Gibbs Williams invited me to be a guest on his internet radio show. Our dialogue led the owner of the station to ask me to start my own program with him, which led to more than 138 audio episodes.

I found the guests for the show in haphazard ways. Some were people I had heard about or knew. Others just showed up on my computer screen in one way or another. Very few turned down the invitation.

📝 Doctor's Notes

This invitation to do a podcast was another step in my current life challenge of accelerating the synchronicity idea into the mind of the general public.

Principle

The still, small voice that comes to you, especially when immersed in nature, can help you prepare for the future. Those soft voices may be offering interesting possibilities. It seems you have to say yes!

PRISON BREAK

Eventually the producer and I became embroiled in a copyright question, so it was time to leave. He kept insisting on being my friend, but the truth is he knew how to manage a naive man. I had to go. But I was at a loss about where to go.

Someone called me to talk about coincidences. Sometimes I answer these calls and sometimes not. It was a man named Mustafa Wahid on the phone. His work as both an academic and entrepreneur caught my attention so I called him back. At the moment I called, he was telling someone about my coincidence work. Mustafa picked up the phone. "That's him?!"

We got deeply into coincidences. I knew that Mustafa was experienced in social media and marketing. He provided the emotional and intellectual leverage for me to switch from the internet radio show to my own YouTube podcast. After that, coincidences with guests seemed to accelerate.

📝 Doctor's Notes

How nice that I called when he was talking about me! This timing jumpstarts and usually strengthens relationships.

Principle

When the need arises, a solution may be on the horizon. Use your intuition, seize the opportunity! Various inputs to intuition can open the gates of synchronicity as we learn to use them through trial-and-error testing. Keep believing in the value of your intuitive messages.

WHITE HAIR AND WHITE MOUSTACHE

The process of finally *not* obtaining the copyright on my internet radio programs was stressful and painful. The producer emailed me that he would give me the copyright, but he slow walked me to a cliff that I had to jump off of into my own podcast.

Why did he own the copyright and not me? Laws too often favor those in power. I found the guests, and I paid him about $50 per episode to record and get each show out on a platform that distributed the show to places like iTunes. However, the law says that the person who records it (puts the content into tangible form) owns the copyright to that tangible form, the recording.

I gave him an ultimatum: give me the copyright or I quit the show. Silence. No more communication from a guy who pretended to be my friend. I am quite naive, sometimes. I too often believe what people tell me about our relationship and their plans to do things with me. We were not friends, and what he said he would do, he did not do. This pattern has repeated for me too many times. To make the pattern even clearer, he removed most of the 138 podcasts I did with him, leaving only those he called my "Greatest Hits," which included only those with the lowest number of listens. Sweet guy.

My non-friend has a distinctive look. A full head of bright white hair and a full bright white moustache. During the time I was jumping off the cliff into my personally produced podcast, I needed physical rehabilitation for an old football injury that had weakened my left thigh. On the way to a physical therapy appointment, I missed seeing an older couple crossing the street and came within a few feet of hitting the man. I looked at their surprised faces (only a few feet from my car window). The man had a full head of bright white hair and a full bright white moustache. No, it was not the producer. He lived a thousand miles away in Canada.

🗒 Doctor's Notes

This coincidence was like a wish-fulfilling dream playing out how angry I was at him. I wanted to scare him but not physically injure him.

How did this coincidence happen? Perhaps my inner GPS got flipped on. I detected this look-alike in the psychospheric radar of my mind and timed the drive to get close but not too close. The dreamlike quality of the near accident illustrates how meaningful coincidences may resemble dreams. Perhaps life is also a dream and sometimes resembles a cartoon show.

—— Principle ——

High emotion (anger) and life stressors (going out on my own) increase the likelihood of meaningful coincidences. Almost hitting his real-world doppelganger was scary (I could have hit him) and satisfying by scaring that doppelganger. Did the producer feel a wave of anxiety?

BROKEN HIPS TIMES THREE

An internet colleague told me that he fell off his roof onto the driveway while trying to put up Christmas lights. He lay there for an excruciatingly long time until someone found him. After many hours, a skilled medical care team helped relieve his intense pain. Sometime before this accident, his elderly mother had broken her hip and also was in a lot of pain, requiring hospitalization. Within two weeks of his accident, his father also broke his hip and contracted Covid-19. The lockdown prevented him from visiting his ailing parents. His mother died before he could tell her goodbye.

📝 Doctor's Notes

Some coincidences are not fun; they are painful and hopefully instructive but nevertheless hard to endure. To quote Claudius in William Shakespeare's *Hamlet* (act 4, scene 5): "When sorrows come, they come not single spies, but in battalions."

—————— **Principle** ——————

Coincidences can be remarkably positive and remarkably awful. Either way, trying to comprehend their possible meaning becomes a challenge for each of us. While it is up to the person experiencing the synchronicity to interpret it, sometimes an external perspective can start the interpretation. My take on this one is that the man needed to pay more attention to the possible negativity he was creating around him. If you have an idea about the possible meaning of a dramatic coincidence involving someone you know, at least offer it to get the person thinking about it again. He was not available for this discussion.

THE WANNABE ROCK STAR MEETS CYCLICAL VOMITING SYNDROME

I wanted to be a rock star. I started looking for people to "sing my book," to put tunes to some of the stories and make an album that could then form the basis of a rock opera based on synchronicities. I asked my good friend jazz trumpeter and university music professor John D'earth to help me. We got a beautiful start on the project, but then he backed out. He had too many other things to do.

John introduced me to the elegant Italian musician Francesco Ronchetti to convert some of the stories from the book *Connecting with Coincidence* into songs. After discussing the melodies and lyrics on a downtown park bench, Francesco developed the stories into full-blown songs. We then needed a sound engineer to convert five songs into radio-ready tunes.

Mark looked like our man. He had the sound equipment and the experience. He knew the business. He brought in excellent instrumentalists to record the guitar, bass, piano, and other instruments, putting all the lines together in very musical arrangements. He graciously settled arguments I was having with Francesco about the musical introduction to the song about my father and me simultaneously choking 3,000 miles away.

Mark told me about his medical problem. Since childhood, he had had episodes of uncontrolled vomiting, sometimes lasting for hours and days. His parents took him to the Mayo Clinic and several other places. No one knew what to do.

Mark would show up in emergency rooms dehydrated, in deep distress, asking for narcotics. The ER people thought he was a narcotics abuser in withdrawal. Narcotics sedated him, relieving his anxiety and slowing down the pain of incessant vomiting. The staff usually discharged him with nothing.

Eventually Mark found a paper describing what he was suffering from: Cyclical Vomiting Syndrome (CVS). I asked him if the name of the author of this paper was David Fleischer. He thought it was.

I had worked with David Fleischer on CVS at the University of Missouri. David had contacted me because CVS looked like a panic disorder variant, and I had done research on panic disorders. I had treated a few patients with CVS and had consulted with David about others.

🗒 Doctor's Notes

Cyclical Vomiting Syndrome is rare. A psychiatrist studying panic disorder in medical patients is rare. A psychiatrist wanting to make an album from stories written in a book about coincidences is also rare.

I thought it meant that when we were finished, Mark might become my patient. Although I offered, he did not take me up on it.

--- **Principle** ---

Amazingly, unlikely synchronicities do not necessarily lead to any outcome. They just are. They can illustrate the strange interconnections we have with others. They demonstrate that synchronicities are not commands. They are suggestions. We decide.

FINDING A PUBLISHER FOR THE SECOND COINCIDENCE BOOK

Writing a book is often like throwing yourself out into a wide-open space and wondering/hoping that something good will happen—positive uncertainty. The coincidence predisposing dynamics of high emotion, life stress, and need are at play in these next three publishing-related coincidences.

My agent, Lisa Hagen, could not find a publishing company for my next coincidence book, which came to be titled *Meaningful Coincidences*. It seems my first book had not sold enough copies to interest a big-time publisher. The game, I learned, was to sell at least 10,000 books before trying to pitch a big time publisher with your next book. The publisher of *Connecting with Coincidence* did not want it—too academic, they said—and suggested I send it to an academic press. Oxford University Press was interested but balked at the telepathy inclusion. What now? No options.

Sky Nelson Isaac had authored two books relating synchronicity and physics with North Atlantic Books. What about that publishing house?

Patrick knew that the founder and publisher of North Atlantic Books, Richard Grossinger, had recently moved to Inner Traditions in Rochester, Vermont. Lisa, who did not know about Richard's change, arranged a zoom call with Richard, Patrick, Lisa, and me. A day later Richard, now an acquisitions editor for an imprint at Inner Traditions, emailed us that he had accepted the book.

📝 Doctor's Notes

Swinging from vine to vine to find a publisher worked.

--- **Principle** ---

To keep swinging from metaphorical vine to vine requires believing the next vine will appear close enough for you to grasp. Keep swinging, if that is your style. As you can tell, it is one of my styles. Keep moving. Keep looking to grasp. Keep looking for something to grasp!

The Fractal Spiral Points the Way

As *Meaningful Coincidences* was getting close to being finalized, I went to bed wondering who I should ask to write the foreword. Many names popped up in my head. How about the psychologist who knows fractals so well, Terry Marks-Tarlow? The book could use a little more about the fractal-like nature of meaningful coincidences.

With my input, the publisher decided on a cover. I wanted a spiral galaxy in the sky and a nautilus (snaillike shell) in the ground to show that spirals exist in galaxies and on earth. As above, so below. They said it looked too much like a biology book. Ok. But they compromised. The sky on the final book cover is dominated by the golden spiral, which is derived from fractals through the Fibonacci sequence. The spirals of spiral galaxies and nautilus shells are real-world examples of the golden spiral. That was another vote for fractal aficionado Terry Marks-Tarlow.

While continuing to obsess about the foreword, I was reading the novel *Magician's Land*. I came to a section about a botanist who was looking at a weird plant on the page of a very old document. He says, "The leaf arrangement looks chaotic, but it isn't. It follows a mathematical sequence. Usually Fibonacci or Lucas . . ." So this mention of Fibonacci as I was reading this magical book further supported the idea that I should ask Terry to write the foreword to *Meaningful Coincidences*. She agreed.

There's more spiraling.

I usually start my podcast episodes with a coincidence story, often one of my own. I was telling this book-cover fractal story at the beginning of my podcast interview with Ray Grasse in September of 2022. While I was telling it, he told me a little later that he was thinking about the fractal image that was to go on the cover of *his* new book. As he thought about this image and listened to my book cover story, the graphic designer for his new book *When the Stars Align* texted him to ask him where to place the fractal on his book cover.

📝 Doctor's Notes

This coincidence series included (1) The decision of my publisher to put the fractal-based golden spiral on my book cover, (2) then my reading the paragraph in the novel as I was thinking about Terry's fractal interest, and (3) Ray Grasse, who not only was having a fractal on his book cover but was being called about its placement while I was interviewing him.

—————————— **Principle** ——————————

The timing of some coincidence sequences strengthens the confirmation of a decision. And they are often also entertaining, as this one was.

12
Literary Coincidences

WHILE WRITING *MEANINGFUL COINCIDENCES*, I was in the midst of a flurry of words, and other people coincidentally joined me in the word *swirl*.

THE DANISH POET

Julie Mariel is a Danish anthropologist and therapist. When I saw an interesting paper of hers on an academic website, I emailed her an invitation to be a guest on my podcast. Six months later she noticed it and accepted the invitation.

Her research with the psychedelic ayahuasca and its correlated synchronicities blossomed into an episode of my podcast.

Julie told me about her twin sister running into a friend named Johan in South Africa; the twins had known him briefly in Bosnia where they were studying the pyramids. Johan then linked Julie to an ayahuasca group in Holland where she would do the field work necessary for her master's degree in anthropology.

During one ayahuasca ceremony, Julie reported that a woman was seeing butterflies between Julie's heart and Julie's beloved Jurriaan without knowing that Julie and Jurriaan were in a relationship. Julie also reported telepathic events that she witnessed or heard of during the ceremony. One person had visions of cancerous lungs and then saw musical notes moving on a page saying DAD, which alerted him to contact his estranged father who he discovered was sick with lung cancer.

I became more curious about Denmark and found a cartoon on YouTube called the *Danish Poet*.[1] In the cartoon, the Danish poet took a boat to visit Sigrid Unset, the 1928 Norwegian Nobel Prize-winning author who had written a three-volume romance novel and whom the fictional poet idolized. A few days after I had empathically traveled to Norway through this clever, funny cartoon, one of my patients was telling me how he and his wife had found a good way to share experiences. They were reading together the three-volume novel of Sigrid Unset. He was currently reading the first volume and she was reading the second. What?!

I told my friend Julie about this; she had never heard of the Norwegian author. A few weeks later she sent me a photo of the Sigrid Unset book displayed in the window of a secondhand bookstore in Aarhus, Denmark.

All three of us, each in our own way, had found the same book by this Norwegian author.

📝 Doctor's Notes

My patient and Julie and I connected to each other through a Nobel Prize-winning Norwegian author. Here is an example of the artistry of meaningful coincidence to be enjoyed in the moment; it highlights how our minds can be connected through the mental internet of the psychosphere.

Principle

Where you focus your attention increases the likelihood that you will see synchronicities bearing the content of what is passing through your own mind.

THE SPACE BETWEEN WITH MICHELANGELO

Bethany Butzer, Ph.D., wrote the paper "Does Synchronicity Point Us toward the Fundamental Nature of Consciousness?" which appeared

---

1. Natália Fašánková, "The Danish poet (2006)," YouTube website, August 23, 2013.

in the *Journal of Consciousness Studies*. As happens when people are focused on understanding synchronicity, meaningful coincidences increase. Butzer provides some remarkable illustrations. Here is one:

An additional example of synchronicity is related to the actual writing of this paper. I originally wrote this paper as an essay for a course that I took on scientific approaches to consciousness. After I submitted my essay, one of my classmates asked if I would be willing to exchange essays with her, because she was interested in seeing an example of my writing. I had never had any personal contact with this student before, and she did not know what my essay was about (we were allowed to write our essay about a broad range of topics—none of which explicitly mentioned synchronicity). We exchanged essays, and a few hours later she sent me an email asking me to open her essay and look at appendix A. I did, and noticed a picture of Michelangelo's painting of God and Adam from the Sistine Chapel. As you will soon see, the final sentence in my paper makes reference to this exact painting, and ties it into the concept of synchronicity. What are the odds that two essays, written by students who did not know each other, for a course that had nothing to do with art history, would both reference this painting? What are the odds that one of the papers would make a (some would argue) strange inferential leap by tying this painting to synchronicity? And what are the additional odds that these two students would exchange essays in order for this synchronicity to be recognized?

What is truly fascinating is that this "Michelangelo" synchronicity did not end there. When I submitted this paper to an academic journal, one of the anonymous peer reviewers responded by noting that five days before reviewing my paper, he had experienced a strong mental image of Michelangelo's painting of God and Adam. He had been contemplating how he came to study coincidences, and was wondering whether his interest was linked to something specific about himself, or to fate. The image of Michelangelo's painting appeared in his mind's eye, and reminded him that it was the combination of these two factors that was important. In his words, "I am striving upward to meet what is coming downward, as in the painting."[2]

📝 Doctor's Notes

I was that reviewer! I had recently imagined the same image Bethany had described in her paper. We would not have discovered it had the editor of the journal *not* selected me as a potential reviewer. Precognition? Tapping into information in the psychosphere? "It's all random" or the hard-to-comprehend theories of God/Universe/Source/quantum field/ fractals? The result was a fascinating interview with Bethany on my podcast.[3] The synchronicity meaningfully connected us.

Principle

Meaningful coincidences illuminate the invisible currents that connect and unify us. It's more evidence for the internet of the mind in the psychosphere.

---

2. Bethany Butzer, "Does Synchronicity Point Us toward the Fundamental Nature of Consciousness? An Exploration of Psychology, Ontology, and Research Prospects," Journal of Consciousness Studies 28, nos. 3–4 (2021): 29–54.

3. Connecting with Coincidence, "Bethany Butzer: Invisible to Visible," YouTube website, August 20, 2021.

13
Internal GPS

SIMULPATHITY, AS EXEMPLIFIED BY the simultaneous choking of my father and me, suggests we can pick up the positive feelings of others in similar subtle ways . . . even their location in space.

STROLLING TOWARD THE FOREST ENTRANCE

Diane and I had danced together a few times before Covid-19 struck. She liked my creds—psychiatrist, synchronicity student. During our first actual conversation on Zoom, the energy exploded between our minds. We cautiously acknowledged each other in little ways in the subsequent months.

She is a fantastic visual artist who was drawing easy-to-understand diagrams of some of the many complexities in human relationships. Since I've written about psychotherapy, I wanted to see some of these ideas drawn rather than written.

In the past she had an encouraging professional relationship with a man who promised to pay her well for her paintings and make her famous. He failed miserably. She was deeply hurt by his neglect and nastiness. Each ended up hiring lawyers to help fight it out. His profession was psychiatry. His first name was Bernard. Bernard the Psychiatrist—just like me! We both hoped that our collaboration would yield more productive outcomes. (It did not, but at least there were no lawsuits.)

Just as I was finishing a draft of this story, which I intended to send to Diane, my phone signaled a text message. The message was from

Diane wishing me a happy Thanksgiving, being so grateful for our friendship. More connection evidence.

🗒 Doctor's Notes

I asked the highly respected statistician David Hand what he thought about Diane texting as I was about to send her the draft. He wrote: "The apparent coincidental nature of it is that one singles out 'the minute after you stop writing' rather than any other single minute: the 60 minutes starting an hour after you finish writing all look much the same. If you singled out beforehand the minute which was three hours after you finished writing and she happened to text you during that minute, you'd again say 'what a coincidence.' It would be just as improbable, but not very interesting. All minutes are equally probable in a random universe. The timing does not suggest a potential explanation."

Please notice that David does not take into consideration the time interval between the two events. The closer the two events are in time, the less probable the coincidence is. Any accurate probability estimate needs to take the time interval into consideration.

Principle

This confluence of events illustrates telepathy. Does it exist? The scientific data are pretty strong. My model requires two fundamental assumptions: (1) the existence of the psychosphere, and (2) each of us has a Higher Self floating around in the psychosphere.[1]

A HUMAN GPS EXPERIMENT

In 2019, I tested out my ability to get where I wanted to be at just the right time. Without calling or texting ahead, I planned to show up at the houses of M and C right when each of them came out of their house.

---

1. Connecting with Coincidence, "How Thought Transference Happens," YouTube website, July 30, 2023.

For M, an intuitive voice I trusted suggested I drive to her house now. I had not seen her in several weeks, and we had rarely communicated by social media or texting. It was 10:00 p.m. and dark. I stopped my car and looked. I saw no activity. As I was about to leave, she stepped out of her car, having gone there to get something just a few minutes before. We talked. Yes! Here was evidence that I could intentionally use my internal GPS.

For C, I decided that before going to her house, I would stop in front of four different houses that I regularly visited. An intuitive voice instructed me when to leave each house. Several times I had thoughts saying "stop, this is stupid." But the voice encouraged me to continue. After the fourth house, I made a wrong turn, even though I had been on this route before. I pulled up at C's house. Her car was there, so she was probably at home. I waited about one minute and then saw her get into the driver's side. I knocked on the window. We spoke briefly. Then she left for a meeting for which she was late. It was further evidence for intentionally using my internal GPS. Her lateness to the meeting permitted this coincidence to take place.

📝 Doctor's Notes

Being in the right place at the right time happens often subconsciously. Randomly sitting down next to someone or arriving late or following an intuitive nudge or getting lost can yield amazing results. Out of the mist of uncertainty, a needed job, person, thing, or idea appears. This experiment suggests that our Internal GPS ability can be activated consciously and probably practiced.

Principle

Current scientific researchers will continue to explore the mysteries of our expanding universe and the immense curiosities living in the depths of our oceans. A third mystery is the human mind, which deserves far more attention than it is getting. How, for example, do mind and brain connect with each other? Insisting that the mind emerges from the brain has yet to be demonstrated. This idea is more faith than reason. The range of coincidences described in this book point toward innate human capacities worthy of disciplined study that suggest that the brain is a filter for the many energy-ideas floating in the psychosphere.

RAVENS ESCORT

I was visiting my old friend Andrew Weil in the summer of 2019. He was living on Cortes Island, off the coast of Vancouver Island, one of the jewels of Canada's British Columbia. As my friend Dina and I walked down the driveway, four ravens left their perches on the trees alongside the driveway and led the way to his house.

📝 Doctor's Notes

Birds and humans seem to have close connections. There are many stories of birds appearing around the death of someone. While the etymology of the word *omen* is uncertain, the word is often associated with birds in the context of its meaning as a prophetic sign. In ancient cultures, the movements and behaviors of birds were often interpreted as signs of what was to come, and some of these signs were considered omens of good or bad fortune.

Principle

Birds (and many other animals) are more like people than we rational thinkers are taught. Or perhaps we are more like animals than we like to believe.

PREPARING FOR RUPERT

A few days earlier on Cortes Island, I was scheduled to have breakfast with Rupert Sheldrake, prolific author and challenger of materialism with his ideas of morphic resonance and morphic fields. The evening before our meeting, my knowledge of his work seemed too limited for a meaningful conversation. I worried about my ignorance. While wandering on one of the nearby trails, I came across a man sitting on a bench in the darkness. We talked and I confessed my ignorance of Rupert's work. He proceeded to pump me full of good information leaving me confident in meeting Rupert.

📝 Doctor's Notes

He could have been an attendee at Rupert's seminar but I never found out. That fact would make the coincidence more likely, and yet, had I not wandered and begun the conversation, my anxiety would have remained. My internal GPS must have been turned on again. I also had to ask. "The Ask," is an important element in coincidences.

Principle

Keep moving! The more intersections you have with other beings and with things, the more likely meaningful coincidences will take place. Intersections are the fundamental elements of synchronicity.

14
The Coincidence Project

Successful outcomes in romance, health, research, business, and most other areas in which effort is expended toward some outcome seem to involve meaningful coincidences. This principle applies to the ongoing development of The Coincidence Project.

A Trail through the Coincidence Jungle

I needed a coincidence partner, someone to help advance the meaningful coincidence banner. Who? There were many candidates. But no one fit until I anxiously asked Juliet Trail. We had occasionally met for dinner to keep in touch. A year or two after we met, she had left her job at the University of Virginia and was attempting to put together her own nonprofit focusing on increasing world compassion through compassion meditation. Did she have the time and interest? Yes, she did! She is very smart and multitalented, a singer and the one-time leader of a local punk band, expert meditation teacher, highly effective organizer, and very interested in synchronicity. A great match of needs and interests. That was March 2020.

📝 Doctor's Notes

The person I was seeking was also seeking me. She was right in front of me. I just had to ask.

Principle

A worldly lesson told through many different versions advises that you can travel all over the world when what you are seeking is right in front of you at home.

FINDING COINCIDENCE AMBASSADORS

We set about gathering people who were individually promoting the idea and experience of synchronicity and serendipity to create a group dedicated to accelerating awareness of synchronicity in world consciousness. Producing this expectation video relied on serendipity.

By stumbling intuitively around on the internet, listening to people talk about coincidences, talking with friends and acquaintances, I found people to interview on my podcasts. They became potential coincidence ambassadors.

An example: Driving the three hours from Virginia Beach to Charlottesville, I looked for something interesting to listen to on the radio. Nothing. Frustrated, I turned to YouTube and to my amazement heard a well-organized TedX talk by a woman in the Netherlands. She had put together a clear-sighted list of coincidence types. I tracked her down and interviewed her on my podcast. Anne Heleen Bijl later became a wonderful board member of The Coincidence Project bringing optimism, empathy, and numerous amazing coincidence stories.

📝 Doctor's Notes

I imagined a future. I created a mind movie—of the future. I relied on synchronicity and serendipity to help me make it real, to produce this movie. Looking around while moving around is so essential. Expecting help from the unexpected, from ambiguity, from positive uncertainty becomes part of the production process.

Principle

Manifestation is another name for producing mind movies of the desired future. In producing them, recognize your limitations as well as your abilities in 3D reality. Asking for more than you can handle or more than is possible from your environment will lead to disappointment.

THE COINCIDENCE CAFÉ

Juliet culled through the list of guests on my 138 radio shows, learning what I knew and selecting guests who might fit well with the future of our meaningful coincidence work. We were stepping forward one foot at a time. We collected some synchronicity enthusiasts and began video Zoom meetings in September 2020. A year later we had a dedicated group of fourteen Coincidence Ambassadors (CAs) meeting together monthly. The CAs wanted to meet more often, so we initiated the Coincidence Café, which welcomes others wanting to meet with synchronicity fluent people. CA Katrin Windsor, who invented the term Coincidence Café, put these drinks on our imaginary menu: *serendipi-Tea* and *synchroniciTea*.

The Coincidence Project hosts Coincidence Café online via Zoom each month, on the third Saturday, 11:00 a.m.–12:30 p.m. Eastern Time (US). At the Coincidence Café, we explore topics relating to meaningful coincidence, synchronicity, and serendipity with new hosts each month. We make time during each session to share our own stories in small groups, inspired by that month's topic. This event is free and open to the public.[1]

In those early Café meetings, meaningful coincidences fluttered by, helping all of us to more deeply engage the CAs and other participants.

From Café attendee Adele, July 2022: "I had an interesting synchronicity connection with Christine. I was telling her about my precognitive dreams, one in particular, so we got on the subject of how the psyche lives outside of time. I then commented that I not only am

---

1. To participate in the Coincidence Café, register online at The Coincidence Project website.

obsessed with the subject of time but have collected clocks and love watches. I was wearing two. Christine told me that her father was a clockmaker and his business was called Timetraveling Clockworks. How cool is that!"

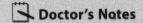 **Doctor's Notes**

Another coincidence delight!

Principle

The primary way to find parallels between people is through dialogue. I encourage you to tell your coincidence stories to relatives and friends to discover the shrouded similarities in each other's life. And join the Coincidence Café.

15
Down by the River

WATER EXPANDS MY MIND. A lake, the ocean, and rivers. The Rivanna River, where many synchronicities seem to flow, runs through the eastern border of Charlottesville.

TWO-PART HARMONY

Lying down by the river one November afternoon, I watched the cloud formations create a horse and rider while I sang. I was ending one of my '50s romantic songs with an extended low tenor note when I heard a harmonic sound drifting down the river, warmly resonating with my note. I looked. Something seemed to be singing with me. It was a vehicle motoring across the nearby bridge.

📝 Doctor's Notes

Immersed in the moment, another part of my reality joined with me in a pleasurable resonance!

Principle

Timing may not be everything, but it sure helps. Immerse yourself in the Now and watch what sometimes happens. Try this: play with the word *nowhere*. The word contains *now* and *here*. You can be immersed in the infinity of Now and be both nowhere and right here now.

GEOMETRIC BUGS

While relaxing by the river's flowing wonder on a Sunday evening, I looked up to see a swarm of bugs zooming about two feet from my nose. Their motions seemed random and chaotic. I looked more closely. Each of them moved in curves. They never bumped into each other. More strikingly, together they formed different shapes that kept changing, partly, it seemed with my increasing trust in them. The more I trusted them, the more relaxed I became with them, the closer they came. Sometimes the shape resembled a sphere, sometimes an ellipse. Despite the apparent individual chaos, they managed to create a stable whole.

So then I challenged them: *Do a spiral*, I silently asked. I love spirals. A few minutes later they had created an upward tunnel with a spiral-like shape inside. Just a coincidence? Or did my mind and their collective mind buzz together?

📝 Doctor's Notes

I believed I could communicate with them. In his first book, *The Natural Mind*, Andrew Weil wrote about communicating with bees. Try believing you can communicate also. I learned to be careful about which ones to connect with. On my hikes in Mint Springs in the summer, some flying insects went for my eyes and occasionally landed in one of them. Irritating!

Principle

Do you want to communicate with insects? It helps to believe you can communicate with them. To me, their apparently random motion was dance-like, coordinated by their individual participation in an unseen unity. Each could be both individual and part of the collective in creating beautiful shapes. Can we together do something like these fliers? Could human beings, with our culturally hardened individuality, create unified shapes while also enjoying the curves of our own personal trajectories? I think we can.

DIFFERENT NAMES FOR GOD

One Sunday afternoon in January of 2023, I was meditating by the river and came up with an answer to this question: Why are there so many names for God? My answer was that most people seem to feel there is a guiding hand, some kind of intelligence that influences us beyond our personal agency. Each culture comes up with its own name for this mysterious influence in each of our lives. The need to name comes in part from the need to feel in control. I thought that the best name of God is The Name, in this way not having to be pinned down to a specific name. The Name could be a name you pick or the name of no name.

I went to another place on the river. I was hoping for an audience for the song I was singing called "Teach Me Tonight." Here are some of the lyrics, the ones I remember.

> *The sky's a blackboard high above you*
> *And if a shooting star goes by*
> *I'll use that star to write "I love you"*
> *A thousand times across the sky*

> *One thing isn't very clear my love*
> *Teachers shouldn't stand so near my love*
> *Graduation's almost here my love*
> *You'd better teach me tonight.*[1]

Two people came down to where I was singing. The woman was taking a photo of the man. I volunteered to photograph both of them. Sensing that they were interested in ideas, I posed the question: Why are there so many different names for God? I suggested that the Hebrew word for The Name, HaShem, would be the best name. They responded by saying, "We are both rabbis." We were quite surprised by the coincidence. We then discussed the question. She thought we need to name God because there is so much outside of our individual control—who

---

1. Jo Stafford, "Teach Me tonight," Lyrics website.

our parents are, where we are born, our genetic structure, and more. By naming, we may feel we gain a sense of control.

So I asked the rabbi at the temple what he thought about this coincidence with the two rabbis and the question I had raised. The week before, he said, the Torah portion (5 books of Moses) read at the synagogue was about how Moses experiences God at the burning bush. Nervous about showing up before the people of Israel with an unnamed God, Moses asks: "What is your name?"

God, in a gentle but firm rebuke to Moses for asking the question, answers: Ehyeh Asher Ehyeh, meaning "I will be what (ever) I will be."

📝 Doctor's Notes

I had apparently picked up the question from the local psychospheric bubble in which the question Moses was asking God was floating around. The rabbis had studied it this past week and I, with my mind flowing with the river, had picked it up too.

Principle

Even naming the mystery "The Name" is a form of naming. In this passage from the Torah, the answer Moses receives is not a noun but a verb, a verb of continual becoming. "I will be what (ever) I will be."

This answer resonates with the Chinese Tao.

"The Tao that can be told is not the eternal Tao. The name that can be named is not the eternal name. The nameless is the beginning of heaven and earth." This quote is from Laozi's Tao Te Ching. It is one of the most important texts in Taoism, and it speaks to the idea that the true nature of the universe and reality cannot be accurately described through language. Names cannot capture the vastness.

WHAT TIME IS IT?

One gorgeous autumn day in 2022, I was walking back to my car after a rest by the river, when I saw up ahead a woman in a wheelchair with her back to me and a woman next to her. I was wondering about what time it was and flirted with the idea of asking them. Right as I walked by them, near enough now to hear, the attendant woman said, "It is 4:36, and we will go in fifteen minutes."

📝 Doctor's Notes

It was as if they heard my projected question out to them. Or did I sense that they would be talking about the time. Or both?

──────────────── **Principle** ────────────────

Once again, away from crowds, houses, technology, with trees and rivers around us, our minds become more open, more able to pick up information and energy from our surroundings, including from other people. Let nature open your mind.

THE NICE FIT

The friend of a good friend of mine has spastic cerebral palsy. I wondered if a good chiropractor could loosen him up, but that seemed unlikely. As I was walking along the river, I saw five men sitting on the rocks. Four of them were listening to the fifth talk. So I said to them that they reminded me of a Grateful Dead song. "What song?" One asked. So I sang the first line of "Uncle John's Band"—"Come hear Uncle John's Band, by the riverside." They laughed and invited me to join them. The speaker, whose name was Rob, turned out to be a bodyworker who was looking for someone with severe spastic cerebral palsy to work on. He had had some success treating mild spastic cerebral palsy. My good friend was delighted to hear of this possibility, but Rob has yet to go see him.

My relationship with Rob evolved. He did bodywork on me for once a week, for about one year. He says that he loosens connective tissue, freeing the body to be looser. I feel looser!

📝 Doctor's Notes

As we age, connective tissue tightens. His eclectic form of bodywork loosens the sheaths around muscles, enabling them to expand, become stronger. Tendons and ligaments also tighten. With his strong hands, they are also loosened.

------------------------------ **Principle** ------------------------------

This is another example of strong serendipity—finding something you are not looking for, but when you see it, you recognize its value. (Weak serendipity is finding something you are looking for but in an unexpected way.)

Once again with feeling—The dog that trots about finds the bone. I'll add, especially when that puppy sniffs around a butcher shop. In this case the "butcher shop" was the Rivanna River where, in my experience, coincidences are more likely to happen. I identify with the flow of water, with the movement of water away from the structures of streets, cars, and rules. Open, nonlinear, non-digital spaces provide freedom for more intuitive movements that open up our internal GPS to create potentially meaningful intersections with other people, plants, animals, butterflies, bugs, and other sentient creatures. Research evidence shows that free movement in stimulus-rich environments increase serendipities.[2]

A Voice Leads to a Book Launch Party

I was sitting among some trees along a little path away from the river, wondering if I should go right, which leads back to the parking lot, or left, which leads to an open area. The thunder was getting louder, the darkening sky a harbinger of rain. As I considered the two options, I heard a voice saying, "Go left." I said to the voice, "Why?" The voice said, "You will see."

So, I went left and started to hear music. Great! I was ready to dance. Someone was doing a sound check on the outdoor stage. It was Devon Sproule, a talented local singer-songwriter whom I had wanted to see. She was going to open in the first set. However, the ticket person told me that

---

2. Lennart Björneborn, "Three Key Affordances for Serendipity: Toward a Framework Connecting Environmental and Personal Factors in Serendipitous Encounters," *Journal of Documentation* 73, no. 5 (September 11, 2017): 1053–81.

the concert was sold out, so I was left to linger outside the fence to listen.

Then a woman came over to me, offering a ticket. The ticket taker had told her that I wanted to get in, and the woman had an extra ticket. I met her husband, and the three of us had a great time together, so we went to dinner together the following week. As our dinner ended, they asked me if I wanted to have a party to celebrate the publication of my new book *Meaningful Coincidences: How and Why Synchronicity and Serendipity Happen*. I readily agreed.

📝 Doctor's Notes

I had wanted to see Devon, having heard a lot about her, but had never seen her perform. I had wanted to find a way to publicize my book in my hometown of Charlottesville, and here I was presented with the opportunity. As the voice suggested, I did see. I saw two desired futures become realized.

Principle

The deeper you get into living coincidence flow, the more what you seek will probably come to you. Those voices in your head can be very helpful sometimes, especially when you know you need to listen.

Sometimes a voice can at first offer a great opportunity, but further on down the timeline, negativity results. I stayed with this helpful couple too long and ended up with a vexing problem with my blood pressure caused by the weed they grew in their backyard. Get out when the getting is good! Maureen St. Germain offered this advice to those hearing potentially useful voices. Ask, who are you? Ask, are you from 100 percent pure Source light? Are you filled with God's pure light? She insists that these entities must answer your questions truthfully.[3] Of course there is no science backing up her advice, but she has had plenty of experience!!!

---

3. Connecting with Coincidence, "Waking up in 5D Synchronicity, Maureen St. Germain, EP 269," YouTube website, September 24, 2022.

SPEAKING OF HEARING VOICES

Because hearing voices is not uncommon, I summarize here a post from my *Psychology Today* blog[4] to help you normalize them.

Hearing voices in psychologically normal people tends to be supportive rather than critical and may offer truths with a validity beyond the limits of the ego. Auditory hallucinations are defined as the sensory perceptions of hearing noises without an external stimulus.[5]

Hearing voices that are easily recognized as one's own commonly occurs. Negative self-talk or criticism of oneself by one's inner critic may be the most common. On the other hand, external voices have been reported to provide helpful guidance to normal people. Many historical luminaries were voice hearers, including Socrates and Plato, Joan of Arc, Sigmund Freud, Carl Jung, and Martin Luther King Jr. External voices are reported to increase in frequency after near-death experiences.[6]

Writing in the *Journal of Transpersonal Psychology*, Liester clarifies the distinctions: Nonpathological auditory hallucinations are similar to psychotic hallucinations in that they are heard in the mind rather than in the ears and yet appear to have an external origin. They speak in the experiencer's native language, they may be precipitated by disruptions in ego function, and they may have both beneficial and detrimental sequelae.

Nonpathological auditory hallucinations differ from psychotic hallucinations in that they tend to be supportive rather than critical; they may offer truths with a validity beyond the limits of the ego; they generally enhance personal, interpersonal, and societal functioning; they usually speak in complete sentences or long discourses; and they are not associated with brain malfunctions.[7]

---

4. Bernard Beitman, "On Hearing Voices," Psychology Today website, August 8, 2022.

5. Tanu Thakur and Vikas Gupta, "Auditory Hallucinations," StatPearls (online), National Library of Medicine website, February 13, 2023.

6. B. Greyson and M. B. Liester, "Auditory Hallucinations Following Near-Death Experiences," Journal of Humanistic Psychology 44, no. 3 (2004): 320–36.

7. M. B. Liester, "Inner Voices: Distinguishing Transcendent and Pathological Characteristics," Journal of Transpersonal Psychology 28 (1996): 1–30.

Two Examples

I report two examples of meaningful coincidences between the advice of the voice and the resulting positive outcome from following that advice. They are coincidences because we have yet to understand how following the advice of an external voice leads to a positive outcome. They are meaningful because each led to positive outcomes.

1. The wife of one of my patients was visiting her sick mother in another state. As she was making a turn onto another road, she took the left lane as was indicated. However, she heard a strong, commanding voice that seemed to be coming from someone inside her vehicle telling her to get over in the right lane. There was no one else in the car. She quickly obeyed. Had she stayed in the left lane, she would have been hit by a truck barreling through the intersection.

2. Carolyn from Philadelphia reported this instance: "While waiting for the public transportation bus to Temple University, something very unusual happened. I normally sat on steps adjacent to the bus stop, every day, while waiting. My routine never varied. This one day, I kept hearing a voice in my head telling me to go stand near the sign about thirty feet away. I ignored it for a couple minutes, but it was very insistent. I walked over to the signpost, and not ten seconds later, a flatbed truck with a car on it came careening around the corner, causing the car to fly off and straight onto the steps where I had just been sitting!"

📓 Doctor's Notes

Just as mental health professionals tend to label high-frequency coinciders (coincidence experiencers) "psychotic," we also tend to label voice hearers as psychotic. And so it is with hearing external voices. Pathological diagnoses rely on whether or not the symptoms interfere with daily functions. In these two examples, an external voice saved the lives of the people involved.

<hr>
Principle
<hr>

When psychiatrists are confronted with someone hearing voices, we are trained to call that person psychotic. Have courage! You may be getting some good advice similar to gut feelings and your internal voice. Like synchronicities, the advice may be very helpful or problematic. Discernment required. In these two stories the only option was action. Yes or no. I wonder how many times someone hears a potentially helpful voice and ignores it to their own detriment.

<hr>

A Launch Party Coincidence

A few days before my book launch party, one of the guests experienced a coincidence that involved me. Judith Minter presented this coincidence at the party: "I was having lunch with others in a park when a guy we didn't know came over to us with a wallet and phone he found in the park and asked if he should turn it over to police. He mentioned the owner lived in Afton—where I live, so I asked to look at it to see if I knew him, and I did. He lives on our road. I contacted his wife and said I'd bring it by. On my way I stopped for some business at the bank, but was delayed due to computer glitches, which placed me arriving at their house at the same time as he did, allowing the opportunity to chat. He was ecstatic, called it a 'miracle' that I had his wallet/phone as he had been desperately trying to figure out where he left them. He had also been in the park for lunch. We were both amazed and in awe of the coincidences! Whoa! I told him that I was going to a launch party for a coincidence book and he said, 'Bernie's? He had an office in the same building I had once had.'"

📝 Doctor's Notes

Judith added: "By my count there were five coincidences—both of us in the park; the stranger bringing the wallet/phone to me; the owner lives on our road; the delay at the bank so he and I could chat; and the fact he knows you!"

—————————— **Principle** ——————————

A meta-coincidence—a coincidence party in which a coincidence is described, which in itself was amazing (she lived near where he lived), and then that both people knew me. A coincidence involving a coincidence. The party was for me and the coincidence was a gift of the present to all of us there. So have a coincidence party and see what happens.

16
Flowing in C'ville

TO GET MY BOOK OUT into the collective mind, I was a guest on more than seventy podcasts in eight months. It was quite exhausting for the first months. I also kept my own weekly podcast going and achieved what seemed like minor miracles in getting articles about me into the *Swarthmore College Alumni Bulletin*, the *Wall Street Journal*, and most impactful of all, the front page of the *Los Angeles Times*. That last one rocketed sales of the book.

After the initial energy devoted to publicizing my book and helping The Coincidence Project become a living entity with dedicated board members, monthly cafés, a monthly speaker series, and evolving plans for the future, I became immersed in a continuing flow of meaningful coincidences in the vortex of psycho-spiritual energy that is Charlottesville. Here are a few of them.

I'm Open to Synchronicity Clients

One of my long-time patients had checked all the boxes of what she wanted from therapy. Our relationship began when she was in her third year of college. Over the six years we had known each other, she finally got a decent job she liked, found a boyfriend who held promise as a life partner, lost excess weight by dieting and strenuous exercise, and had a group of good friends. Eventually free time was more important to her than meeting with me. I usually feel some sadness, loss, and sense of abandonment when this happens. But those feelings were outweighed by knowing I had helped her get to a good place in her life.

So since I had an open time, I said to no one in particular: "Please send me a synchronicity patient." Shortly afterward, I was in a meeting on Zoom with two of my patients struggling with making sense of their synchronicities. As is common with people needing coincidence counseling, an onslaught of synchronicities had shaken up their lives by threatening to suggest that reality is not what they have been taught.

📝 Doctor's Notes

We teach to learn. By helping others, we all learn, since their problems can mirror our own. By helping people coming to The Coincidence Project, I become more deeply engaged in the swirling confusion of meaning and emotions evoked by synchronicities.

Principle

The psychosphere, our Earth's mental atmosphere, can convey information to those open to receiving it. Just ask and trust whoever or whatever you believe mediates your request.

THE TIMELY EMAIL

This story involves three guests who individually had appeared on my podcast, *Connecting with Coincidence*: Sheila, Josh, and Anna. Anna and Sheila knew each other. Josh knew neither one. As usual, I was sending Sheila the link to our just-published interview. I then felt a nudge, a small urge to copy Anna on the email, justified by the fact that Sheila and Anna were practicing psychiatrists in Connecticut with an interest in synchronicity. Very quickly afterward, I received a voice mail from Anna (which I paraphrase): "Thanks for copying me on this email! Guess who I am dancing with now. Yossi! (Josh). I'm in Los Angeles at a dance talking with Josh (whom she had never met before). We started talking about synchronicity and Josh said he knows Bernie Beitman, the founder of synchronicity. I say that I was on his podcast and am a friend of his as well. As I was saying that, your email arrived. I just had to call and tell you that synchronicity."

📝 Doctor's Notes

The urge in me completed this unlikely synchronicity. Of the many people at dance, Josh and Anna found each other. They had never met before. Then they start talking about synchronicity and then about me. And just when I sent the email, they were talking about me.

It was enough that two strangers met to talk about synchronicity and me. Then add that I may have picked up this unlikely conversation through the psychosphere and acted upon the urge that registered in my conscious mind and encouraged me to copy Anna about a synchronicity interview with Sheila.

Principle

A coincidence involving a coincidence is a meta-coincidence. This coincidence category often makes minds swim in amazement—another example of telepathy through the psychosphere.

A COINCIDENCE WARNING

I love dancing. Here in Charlottesville our free-form dance is based on five rhythms, starting slow, going fast, and ending slow. We move however we feel. Things happen on the dance floor. Energy gets exchanged, feelings aroused, connections made. About a year ago, a wonderful new dancer appeared and slowly over time, we danced. It was wonderful. And so it continued. My heart opened up to her. She asked me to go for a walk with her. I readily agreed, knowing that outside the dance floor, relationships can be treacherous. I suggested a time and day. I also texted her that I did not want to get hurt again. She said she would never hurt me. So, okay.

Turns out she loves poetry and sent me one she was working on. The title: "All Relationships End in Heartbreak."

The coincidence of my fear of being hurt and this poem served as a warning to me: do not proceed. Did I heed the warning? Yes! Bolstered by the advice and support of several friends. That walk did not happen.

Follow-Up: Afterward, I did ask her to dance, twice, and each time I asked, she dismissed me like the strand of her hair she once plucked off my shirt. I felt a little hurt, but just a little. Those small rejections became vaccines against the pain of future hurts. Eventually, we began our occasional full-of-wow dancing again. I recognized that she needed to be the one who initiated the dance. Each dance was complete in itself, even when she ended a dance with "to be continued." The beat goes on.

⌐ Doctor's Notes

Am I too sensitive? Yes. Have I misjudged relationships before? Yes. Did I miss the early signals in previous relationships that things were not going to work out as I may have wanted them to? Yes. It was liberating to overdo protecting myself so that if and when a new possible romance begins to bloom, I will be careful but not overly careful. I will be open but not naively hoping for an unrealistic romantic development.

Principle

Coincidences can not only be suggestions, they can be warnings about an impending decision.

Monkey Bars

While editing this compilation of personal coincidence stories, I started to notice patterns. One of them, as you may remember, is *swinging from vine to vine in the coincidence jungle.* This means that I grab a vine, swing into unknown space, trusting that there will be another vine to grab to go on to the next tree.

A few days after this pattern had become even clearer, one of our donors to The Coincidence Project, Ann, told me that she thinks of her life as swinging on the monkey bars in children's playgrounds. I had used this same analogy but then expanded it to the vine in the coincidence jungle on the playground of reality.

I'd never heard anyone recognize this monkey-bar pattern in their coincidences.

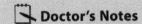
Doctor's Notes

This jungle gym coincidence with Ann further strengthened our relationship. She has been the primary donor to The Coincidence Project.

--- **Principle** ---

Embrace the mirrors of your mind that coincidences can often be. These glitches in the matrix can be clues about what is going on now and what is going to happen. If Ann and I like the monkey bar image for our coincidence experiences, then there are many other people using the same metaphor.

17
Interpersonal Energy

A COINCIDENCE IS an unlikely, surprising, and unexpected intersection of two apparently unrelated events with no apparent explanation. Interpersonal energy qualifies as a meaningful coincidence because it is surprising and unexpected. But once interpersonal energy is accepted as a real part of life, it will no longer be a coincidence.

Trust, comfort, and mutual respect contribute to the success of psychotherapy. Early in my career as a psychotherapist, I noticed the waxing and waning of my connections with different patients. Within this therapeutic alliance, I felt changes in the intensity of the energy, which ebbed and flowed like tides coming in and out. It felt as if there were a dynamic electromagnetic cylinder that expanded and constricted between us. I could feel it on my skin, sometimes penetrating into my body, and occasionally into my heart. (Your skin is your largest sense organ. Only your eyes process more sensory information.)

My training does not allow me to believe my senses, so I wanted to find a physiologist who might know how to measure this interpersonal energy field. I knew about Kirlian photography, which imaged electromagnetic fields, also called auras, around people. It turns out that electrophysiologist Valerie Hunt, the author of *Infinite Mind: The Science of Human Vibrations*, has demonstrated the existence of human bioenergy. While a medical student on a summer research grant in Los Angeles, I saw an aura around a person performing on a stage, so I knew visually that some kind of energy field existed. And years later at the Monroe Institute near Charlottesville, I met physician Brian Dailey who takes brilliant photographs of these electromagnetic fields.[1] But none of them show the dynamic interpersonal effects I sought to substantiate what I sensed.

I don't need a scientific measuring device to tell me when the sun is warm. Or to know the coolness of an icy wind. I register the warmth and the coolness by differences in skin sensations. Similarly, I don't need a scientific measuring device to tell me that interpersonal energy exists. I feel it on the skin of my face and body and the up-and-down sensation waves in my heart. Yet I would like additional conventional evidence.

THEN CAME DANCE

On hot summer days, I would often do a sweaty hike at Mint Springs and then dive into the lake there. One day, I started talking with a woman, Sophia, playing with her son, whose name is Phoenix. The night before I had heard a local band called Phoenix Noir. This name coincidence led to an interest in each other. After several lovely times together, there was a semblance of something between us.

One day she invited me to her older son's birthday party in a converted barn in the countryside outside Charlottesville. A DJ was spinning a playlist, and there she was elegantly tripping the light fantastic on the shiny hardwood floor. I tried out my football-baseball-rugby-tennis playing body, slowly recalling the psychedelic-fueled free-form dance of my hippie days. *Move to the rhythm, feel the beat, move with the flow, become the music!* I needed the nodding approval of the ten-year-old birthday boy that I was doing ok out there. Thank you, Mike.

Paul the DJ then turned me on to the C'ville Dance Co-op. Every Friday evening and Sunday morning, someone brings a playlist, and everyone dances for ninety minutes. We do what feels right, we let our bodies express themselves, a meditation in motion, while also feeling the vibrations of the group.

I am older than most of the dancers, whose ages range from about twenty to fifty, some with children, and some older like me. At first I

---

1. Take a look at Brian Dailey's Facebook page titled "Energy Medicine Squared."

felt awkward, socially intimated by all the people. I was certain that someone would tell me to leave and not come back, and worried that I couldn't dance right.

Now, several years later, I am one of the regulars who help new people feel comfortable there, encouraging them to return.

In between, there have been many interpersonal dancing adventures. The feel of the dance culture resembles the hippie heaven we felt in the San Francisco of the late 1960s. It was back again and happening now. No talking on the dance floor. So deliciously silent from human speech. Just the music. Just the music, which most of the time had no vocals, just instrumental. That's the scene.

Misty Mawn and Bernie at Dance, Charlottesville, VA.

Life for me is an adventure in figuring out how reality works. I am an anthropologist making mental notes about what's happening, and then trying to remember well enough to write some of it down.

At dance, I confirmed the hypothesis that was developing with my patients. Interpersonal energy became yet more real. The experienced dancers know it is real. They play with it, go with it, generate it, and surf on it. They could vigorously dance and not feel drained, just keep going. When dancing with someone or by yourself, you search for the sweet spot between intense focus and gentle noninvolvement. Not too rigid and not too loose. In that sweet spot, the energy moves us, and we move with the energy. Dancers are drawn to other dancers emanating positive energy. When I get in the groove and become part of the music, I can sometimes open my eyes to see who is feeling the energy emanating from me.

Yes, the energy around someone can't be seen most of the time, but when you become sensitive to its existence, when you believe, know, feel that it exists, you can almost see it. Some dancers are encased in their solid boundaries, dancing in their own iron bubble. Some of them are open and invite others to connect with them. Many undulate between the two.

LAURA LEE ON FIRE

On Sunday, August 8, 2021, I dragged myself to dance partly because when I don't feel like going, something really fun often turns up. My thighs were aching from some vigorous dancing twelve hours previously.

At first, it was hard to get the energy up, even though the music was good. My enjoyment of the music varies with the person in charge of the playlist. Some of them put on these bang, bang, bang, electronic drumming songs that feel like an assault to me, so I leave until those songs are over. Then Laura Lee, my friend of many years, shows up with her red hair, blue eyes, and smile. I briefly move near where she is sitting on the floor. We say something to each other, and suddenly I am energized. Really? Yes! I get up and move. No heavy thighs, no droopy motion. I was going! I helped form a circle with three other dancers including Laura Lee and we go.

After dance, I tell Laura Lee how nice it was to be energized by her. She says, "I am on fire, watch out you might get burned." I report the great feeling and then ask her what's contributing to it? "I'm in active flow mode right now," she says, "with a lot of teaching and creating."

📝 Doctor's Notes

This direct experience of an energy infusion right there on the dance floor was confirmed by Laura Lee.

Principle

Dance can be like a gas station where you can fill up on energy from others who have extra energy to express and exchange. Your energy may also feed them.

ENERGY CLOUDS

After three intense dances with three different women on three different evenings, weeks apart, I slept through each subsequent night immersed in their energy. These energy clouds were like perfume from each woman permeating my being. Each cloud was their essence, vibrating unacknowledged senses in me and clinging to those senses. Energy generated by them, enveloping me, inundating my being. By morning, their vibrating essences, each with different feelings, had evaporated into the light. One of them later told me that she had invoked the Divine Feminine between us. Another had deliberately cast this spell to hook me into writing a recommendation letter for her psychiatric residency.

In the middle of 2021, further evidence for these energy clouds emerged. Dances with three other women ended with tears in their eyes. One told me later she had been moved by what we had created. Each subsequent time we saw each other, we were quickly in each other's arms, as if our energy fields shared a deep, familiar resonance. The second said she had never let someone touch her like that at dance.

Afterward, she avoided me on the dance floor. The third person began sobbing while we were dancing so that after the music stopped I felt the need to hold her close until her sobbing subsided. For several months she also avoided dancing with me. My therapist guessed that their vulnerability frightened two of them. The first one simply wanted more hugging: "The best hugging I've had in years," she said.

📝 Doctor's Notes

Without my realizing it, three women immersed me in their energy clouds and three other women joined me in a shared energy cloud.

Principle

Experienced dancers know that dance floor energy exists. Outside of dance, the intensity and form can vary. Listen to athletes describe how they feed off the energy of the crowd. They know it is real. Open yourself up to the possibility.

Leslie Greiner, synchronicity co-presenter, and Bernie.

CHI WHIZ! ENERGY EXCHANGES
DURING PSYCHOTHERAPY

Scientists are studying the movement of energy from healers to patients. But no one seems to have developed a device that can measure the ebb and flow between people. If you know of devices that can measure interpersonal energy, please let me know.

Interpersonal energy is distinct from the commonly acknowledged nonverbal communications like facial expressions, body language, and modulations in voice tone. Most people do not consciously register this energy but are nevertheless affected by it. Four common responses to the energy of another person are feeling energized, rattled, neutral, or drained. 'Creeped out" is what a dance friend called the experience of dancing with a man who repeatedly crossed boundaries with other women and some men.

Have you ever felt unusually energized around a certain person? Do some people drain you? Try paying attention to the ebb and flow of these unseen vibrations in your social life. At a gathering, is there someone in the room who draws people to them like a warm fire on a cold day, not because of attractive appearance but because of some vibrating positivity?

I ask myself about energy with each psychotherapy patient I see. My in-person office is an experimental lab, a controlled setting, where I have the opportunity to experience and observe the varying effects different people have on me. I sit in the same chair. The patients sit on the same small couch. We look at each other from similar angles—almost but not quite straight on. They talk. I listen. I get to feel their energy impact on me. And they may feel my energy impact on them. I feel the waxing and waning of connection. Surprisingly, these energy fluctuations can also be felt through virtual online sessions. Some people drone on in self-involved word productions without reaching out to me with their biofield energy Others engage their biofield with me while they speak.

When we are connected, I continue to see a tube of energetic intensity between our minds and feel the energy connecting our hearts. The tube is surrounded by lesser gradients of energy. The energies fluctuate.

HIGH INTERPERSONAL ENERGY

In one in-person session, I helped a woman in her early twenties embrace her romantic feelings for women. The following week, several different young men asked her out for dinner. She had never experienced this many dinner date requests before. An anomalous week? Previously she had been asked not for dinner, but to "come to my apartment" in early morning texts from drunk, sexually driven guys. She accepted some of these offers.

She began to realize that she had an extraordinary magnetism. In bars, highly accomplished male athletes and some aggressive women hit on her. She does not consider herself to be particularly beautiful or sexy looking. So they are not attracted by her looks. There is something else. She seems to have learned to "pump up" the biobattery of her body and mind to generate energy that attracts people.

During our next session, she seemed to glow, a warm, positive, life-enhancing energy. It was much stronger than in any previous sessions. She had allowed herself to experience herself in ways she had long repressed.

📓 Doctor's Notes

The details of other people's attraction to her, and her notable energetic effect on me, helped to convince her that she had this amazing biobattery-capacity.

--- **Principle** ---

Try mastering your bioenergy field. It's important to strengthen your energetic boundaries to prevent others from creating negativity in your personal energy field. Meditating on your energetic boundaries can begin to help.[2]

---

2. This guided meditation might help you as it has helped others: Know the Self, "Take Back Your Power + Define Your Container with Amelia Aeon Karris," YouTube website, March 1, 2017.

LOW INTERPERSONAL ENERGY

A thirty-year-old man working as an accountant came into my office weekly. He was a very nice, intelligent person. But he had very low energy. He had been depressed but was not now. He was functioning pretty well with his job and marriage. Yet I had difficulty being with him because he emanated so little interpersonal energy.

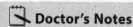 **Doctor's Notes**

I now recognize that I convert the energy from my patients into energetic help for them. We are a team; I need more than their reports. I need some charge. I need them to be engaged with me. When I don't get enough positive charge from them, I must find more energy within me.

Other therapists may not be like me. They may have more energy to give, or they may know how to manage low-energy situations better than I can. Or perhaps they operate primarily on cognition. How far does my experience extend into the work of other therapists? I asked a group of twenty-five therapists whether or not they recognize interpersonal energy with their patients. About half raised their hands. More research is waiting to be done on the energy fields within the psychotherapeutic relationship.

Principle

Psychotherapists need to study the energetic fit between themselves and their patients. When they come home to their partners with their energy lowered, they may actually have given all of it in the office. I think we will need to learn how to more efficiently conserve our energy outputs and keep learning ways to ethically absorb energy from others as well as from nature. Trees help to energize me.

CD PLAYER HAS A MIND OF ITS OWN?

My computer wasn't working and the repair people were being very slow. I let my frustration out by screaming in the car on the way to the repair shop. While I was screaming, my car's six-slot CD player kept jumping from one disc to another. It kept shifting even when I was not screaming. Then, when the computer was fixed, and my frustration reduced, the car CD player stopped jumping around and behaved itself.

📝 Doctor's Notes

I had trouble challenging the belief that my biofield couldn't impact machines. The CD player and the high emotion that sometimes disturbs videoconferencing connections have helped me to change my mind: we can impact machines. For more on how our emotions influence electronic communications please see my discussion with Joe Cambray.[3]

Principle

Human minds are connected to our environment, not only to other people and animals and plants, but also to the machines we use. Many people have observed that video and audio-teleconferencing connections sometime become erratic when intense emotions are sent through the internet. Sometimes it's random, sometimes direct cause and effect. Psychokinetic refers to mind (psycho) moving (kinetic) things.

The existence of fields of energy in and around us has been recognized by philosophical systems around the world: prana (Sanskrit), ruach (Hebrew), pneuma and psyche (Greek), spiritus (Latin). Chi or qi in Taoism refers to universal energy or life-force both outside and inside the body. Hindus refer to Shakti as the surrounding feminine energy and kundalini as its manifestation in the body. Modern day energy workers seem to be working with the same energy fields.

THE WASHING MACHINE OVERFLOWED

A woman I knew from dance, and for whom I felt some affection, put out a request on the dance group email that she needed a place to stay

---

3. Joe Cambray. Emotion distorts zoom signals. YouTube website.

for two months. It was winter 2023. I did not like the idea of her having no place to stay. I had room.

Two months later, she was still in the house. She had overstayed her welcome, but she had no idea that she was no longer a welcome guest. As the energy in the house became increasingly negative, the washing machine overflowed. Never before had this happened in the twelve years I had been in the house. And the machine had been there for at least ten years before I moved in.

A technician declared that there was a small hole in the gasket surrounding the front-loading door. We ran the machine at least ten times, no more flooding. A year later, no flooding.

Also during the time she was staying here, the electrical power to the house was threatened. The panel on the outside of the house now contained corroded connections and needed immediate replacement; otherwise the appliances in the house could have been severely damaged.

Then the internet connectivity to the neighborhood went out.

I anxiously demanded that she leave—her energy was scaring me.

After she left, the lights in the kitchen flickered on and off for about a week and then went back to normal.

Just a set of coincidences?

Doctor's Notes

It took me several weeks to finally get used to the feeling that she was no longer in the house. She is a powerhouse of demanding intensity. The clearest reactions to her presence were the flooding washing machine and the flickering lights when she left. The electrical power and internet connection problems could have been mere coincidences. The source of the problem was likely my chaotic biofield in response to her presence in my house.

Principle

Humans have sufficient energy stores to disrupt mechanical and electrical machines.

18
Deus Ex-Machina

You can't always get what you want. If you try some time,
you just might find, you get what you need.

—The Rolling Stones

PERHAPS I WAS GETTING into deep flow. Or my energy vibration was getting higher, more coherent. Or I was becoming yet more myself. Through a variety of pathways, what I needed arrived.

Anecdotal evidence from The Coincidence Project (TCP) suggests that the immersion in the study and promotion of meaningful coincidences increases the likelihood that meaningful coincidences will occur as part of this creative process. I describe three crucial synchronicities that appeared "out of the blue" just when what TCP needed was offered.

UNEXPECTED MONEY

In November 2022, soon after the incorporation on April 14, 2022, of The Coincidence Project as a nonprofit in the state of Virginia, I received a check in the mail for $1,000 for TCP "to be used in any way you see fit." Our fundraising consultant gave me the donor's contact information. At the end of a thirty-minute conversation, she decided to send us a check for $25,000, which was utterly necessary to get us through the first year.

ONE EDITOR QUITS, A BETTER ONE ARRIVES

I recruited an old friend (the hippie with six signs in Aquarius) to edit the stories sent to the TCP website for publication. She helped to establish the necessary guidelines, and then decided this work was not for her. Two days later on March 31, 2023, I received an email from Ken Bell who could do editing and much more.

CRAWLING OUT ON A LIMB

In March 2023, I offered to do a webinar on Medical Synchronicities for the alumni of Andrew Weil's Integrative Medicine Fellowship at the University of Arizona. The staff were interested and so I was out on a limb. I had plenty of psychiatric and psychotherapy examples. I needed cases from nonpsychiatrists. On April 2, 2023, James Schemmel emailed me out of the blue: "I'm a sixty-two-year-old otolaryngologist. Multiple very interesting Coincidences in my life. Many seem to involve the practice of medicine. What I find most interesting is their impact on my interaction with different patients."

I requested case examples and he delivered two cases that were examples of precognition. Here is one of them:

> On a Sunday morning while reading a book. I had some sort of vision or dream. It came into my mind of a patient I had never met before. The patient was in the hospital at another service. He just happened to have a tracheostomy. The vision or dream that came to me was the patient bleeding from his tracheostomy site with a host of hospital personnel surrounding his bed trying to sort out the situation. That evening around approximately 10:00, I was called to the hospital to see a patient. When I walked into the room, it was the exact same scene that I had witnessed earlier that morning, the same people standing around the patient. It was very peaceful and surreal. I felt no stress or anxiety. Things went extremely smoothly because I had already anticipated the situation.

Yes, even surgeons experience meaningful coincidences.

📝 Doctor's Notes

What you are seeking may also be seeking you (Rumi). Synchronicities like these reflect our connections to people we don't know with whom we share a potential glove-in-hand relationship—their glove fits our hand. Our need activates their need to serve, to help.

Principle

How need manifests the sought response can be understood through the metaphor of the internet. You put in your request for needed information and a series of algorithms finds matches. The specificity of your request helps sharpen the results. I propose that parallel processes take place between your energized, emotionally charged thoughts and the "glove" wanting to cover your hand. Their specific energy-information signatures complement each other and draw them to you through the psychosphere, through this sparkling mental internet.

We need further study about the conditions that increase these connections. Gratitude, need, openheartedness seem to be necessary. Petition prayer and being in the flow of evolving yourself seem to also increase the likelihood. Most importantly, be ready to see what you need when it appears.

GOINGS ON IN GOA

A friend from dance was travelling around India. In Goa, which is in eastern India, she saw a man with a tee shirt saying Mr. Synchronicity on it. She asked him, "Do you know Dr. Coincidence?" He said, "You mean Dr. Beitman?" He was from England and was also traveling around. She was amazed.

📝 Doctor's Notes

Had she not known my dual identities she could not have asked the man about the possible connection. We re-cognize things. Re = again. Cognize = think. Think again.

Principle

A subset of humanity is becoming increasingly interested in synchronicity. My friend told me that India "is full of them."

THE ORIGIN STORY OF DR. COINCIDENCE

I grew up reading Superman and Batman comics. Each of these heroes had a dual identity. I thought that having two identities was normal. One identity was conventional and the other had superpowers. I preferred Batman. Replace the first *a* in Batman with *ei* and you get Beitman. Our own names sometimes correlate with our self-image and what we do. At one time the fastest runner in the world was Usain Bolt; there is a lawyer named Sue Yoo, a neurologist Lord Brain, a

Dr. Coincidence at a great party, Charlottesville, VA.

gastroenterologist Joshua Butt. There are many more names collected under the category of nominative determinism.[1] Think about your name. Is it related to what you do or your image of yourself?

Traversing life, I usually had two different identities. In high school and college I was a nerdy, excellent student as well as an outstanding athlete. As a psychiatric resident, I was both a trainee and a part-time hippie. Dr. Coincidence emerged through the hippie; Dr. Beitman through academic success. As I write this, Dr. Beitman does his podcast, has a Psychology Today blog, and authors synchronicity books. Dr. Coincidence dances, connects with higher consciousness, and comes up with new ideas about coincidences. They have decided to be partners so that they can work together more effectively.

---

1. "Wanting a career change? Consider your name next time you apply for a job" Icon website article.

19
Communicating with Trees

WHY AM I INCLUDING TREES in stories of meaningful coincidences? Well, when two apparently unrelated events coincide and the coincidence produces meaning, then conversations with trees fit the definition. I talk with trees.

A growing collection of articles and books now celebrate our huge vertical friends.[1] Being around trees may help to lower human mortality.[2]

Some people tell stories of interaction with trees. However, in my reading, there is little mention of the possibility of direct communication with those lumbering giants whose ability to aid us includes not only absorbing carbon dioxide but also absorbing human distress. Their ability to provide shelter hints at their ability to comfort and support.

DOMESTIC AVOCADO TREES

Avocado trees grown from the pits of store bought avocados have been my companions since 1971. The first one flourished in the bay window of my bedroom in the majestic Victorian on Hayes Street in San Francisco. I so loved my first avocado tree that, as I was preparing to leave the City by the Bay for Seattle, I pleaded with a friend to take it

---

1. Richard Schiffman, "'Mother Trees' Are Intelligent: They Learn and Remember," Scientific American website, May 4, 2021.

2. Russell McLendon, "People in Portland Planted Trees. Decades Later, a Stunning Pattern Emerged," Nexus Newsfeed website, November 25, 2022.

back to his home in San Jose to care for it. There was no room in my trailer for the move to Seattle. In Seattle I managed to grow another avocado tree despite the many gray days. That tree eventually made it to Columbia, Missouri, but failed to thrive there.

In Charlottesville a new tree friend sprouted in my consulting office and helped absorb the persistent negative energy that accompanies most people seeking psychiatric help. Only one person criticized the plant—"That's ugly," she said. We did not like that. Eventually she said goodbye to us. She and I conflicted. She did not want to consider my perceptions of her strongly held beliefs.

For the first time in my life with avocado trees, this one tried to bear fruit. Twice! Cute little flower petals dotted the pot and the floor. Hey, I told the tree, "You need more leaves and more sun to power the fruit-making possibilities." The tree nevertheless persisted. And then around the time my second granddaughter was born, the tree lost all its leaves. I was frantic, I did not know what to do. But I learned that avocado trees do that. The tree refurbished itself once more.

A second tree eventually joined the first one in my office. A patient had found two intertwined little trees growing in his compost heap and kindly gave the pair to me. The twins thrived and also helped absorb the intensity of my disturbed and disturbing patients.

The pandemic and my partial retirement required a move of the trees to my house where they flourished, like sun-starved northerners who had been moved to the tropics.

Now the twins and three others are doing pretty well out in my sunroom with windows all around but blocked from direct sun in the summer by the magnificent oak tree outside. In the new locale my original buddy strung out a very long branch along the ceiling. I kept asking why he was doing that as there was no light up there, but he insisted. He then appears to have died, leaving a thick trunk and a strong branch on which the twins lean. Maybe he is still alive because water disappears from his dish. Maybe it's just evaporation. In any case, his spirit remains.

I tell you these avocado stories to let you know of my love of trees.

Maybe this background will help you believe me when I tell you that I talk with trees, and they talk with me.

My affinity for forest trees has a long history.

MOUNT TAMALPAIS

My first conversation with a wild tree took place in the early 1990s on Mount Tamalpais just north of San Francisco. I got lost as dusk was falling, but I didn't know I was lost. I stopped, leaned against a tree, and asked the tree "What are you doing?" I distinctly heard, *I'm standing here.* The communication clearly arose from outside of my own mind. My face scrunched like some befuddled, tricked cartoon character.

Weeks later, I found myself inside a circle of trees at Golden Gate Park and tried to start up a conversation. Nothing. Maybe they had enough humans around them so they were closed off from communication with me.

THE FOREST SPEAKS TO ME

Many years later I found a trail up another mountain, this one near Crozet, Virginia, about twenty minutes west of Charlottesville in the Blue Ridge Mountains.

Mint Springs State Park is a quiet gem in the Virginia countryside. Its many paths traverse the mountainside, including a steep trail to a small cliff overlooking a valley. I would often lie down at the foot of the cliff in a small bower of bliss, surrounded by trees, feeling the shifting breeze, or light rain dotting my face, or the groaning of trees in the wind as my thoughts glided into lovely spaces my memory could not hold.

We grew to know each other, the forest and I. Lying in another place lower down, ants crawled all over me like the tips of the forest's fingers getting a tactile sense of this human body-mind in the forest mind. Although I have laid down many subsequent times, no forest fingers have examined me since.

In 2010, something halted my steady pace. I had bumped into an energy band that extended across the path. The energy band seemed to emanate from a pair of trees. We became acquainted. They became the King and the Queen to me. He was thicker and darker than she. Their upper branches reached for each other. Ever since that first encounter, I have regularly visited them. Our relationship has grown so much that I feel a part of them, and they a part of me. I wish I could tell you more than I can because so many interactions I've had with them are hard to believe. And hard to remember. What, me talking with trees? We share love and affection, deep respect, and continuing depths of understanding.

The King and the Queen are growing near a stream close to a path on the way down the mountain. I always stop to visit with them on my every-other-Saturday hikes. For a long time, I found myself bowing, swaying, and almost kneeling in their presence. And then we telepathed. Later we became occasional equals.

They liked making fun of me. Okay, maybe you don't believe me, but maybe all this commotion about the King and Queen will get you thinking about the consciousness of these wondrous creatures. So, yes, I kept questioning whether I was really talking with them or just projecting my own thoughts onto them. I needed to get evidence that their communications were coming from outside of me. And here I remind you of my inner psychiatrist who cautions me and you: If you think the voices you hear are coming from outside your skull rather than from inside your skull, you are on your way to being called psychotic. That's basic psychiatric thinking. And it may be why you don't want to tell mental health professionals about voices you hear, or your friends or relatives. As I mentioned earlier, many well-known people reported that they heard voices from outside of them, people like Winston Churchill, the prime minister in England. They were not psychotic. So where to draw the line? If you are functioning well, we don't call you crazy, at least most of the time.

The trees knew I was skeptical. So they played a few mind games with me. There was this woman . . . she was for me unreachable, I thought, but I wanted to connect more with her. The trees seemed to know that. So they said, *Which is more believable—that this woman really likes you or you are talking with us?* This question may not strike you the way it struck me. I quickly imagined the two options. It was more likely that I was talking with the trees.

An even more convincing trick they pulled on me involved Laura Lee, the redheaded woman at dance I mentioned previously. During one conversation, they blasted a thought into my mind: *Get that red-head here!* They were referring to Laura Lee who creates graphic novels. The demand came loud and clear from outside my mind. A little bewildered, I meandered down the path toward the stream. On my right, I noticed a fungus with red outlines and a gradually pinker interior. The red was the color of Laura Lee's hair. This coincidence seemed like a way to emphasize their request. I wrote a poem, and with my songwriter collaborator, composed a song commemorating the event. It starts

> *The forest speaks to me*
> *Sometimes through the trees*
> *With ever-increasing crescendo*
> *Calling for Laura Lee*
> *Calling for Laura Lee*

Despite my repeated requests and numerous times of singing those lyrics to her, Laura Lee did not visit the King and Queen. Why did they want her there? After months of cogitation, the answer came. They were tired of my involuted, obsessional, idea-creating mental life. They wanted someone with a visual sense to appreciate how beautiful they are. I have since come to see how beautiful they and the other trees are, how funny sometimes, and how warmly enveloping they can be.

The King and Queen are connected to all the trees through the underground Wood Wide Web. Our conversations seem to reverberate through the mind-like web of fungi filaments entwining their roots below the ground surface.

Sometimes the mind of the forest itself seemed to be talking directly to me—pretty loudly. One time they told me to leave and not come back for six weeks. I had been going there at least every two weeks. Why, I asked? *You have been asking too much from us, too many problems, too much complaining. We need a break from you. You are too self-involved.* I felt like Adam and Eve being kicked out of the Garden of Eden. I cried. I stayed away for six weeks and was very happy to be back, once again feeling embraced by them.

The forest did complain about all the thinking I did, for the same reason they wanted Laura Lee there. I was so caught up in my thinking that I did not notice how beautiful the trees and the forest and the sunlight and colors and the plants and the breeze in the trees were. I had been wondering why I had so many apparently good thoughts while hiking with them. They told me I was a thought-manufacturing machine, and that my thoughts went out into the psychosphere for others including me to pick up later, if so disposed. But enough was enough. They wanted to be appreciated. Over the years since then, I have been able to appreciate the beautiful forms (the limbs of trees make funny and clever shapes), colors (I love their lush green aliveness in spring and the patterns of colorful shapes of their fallen leaves in autumn), and the movements (the wind, the streams, the sounds, the aliveness) of the forest. They got me to do what they needed from Laura Lee. A gift for each of us.

Then they told me to leave for another six weeks. Why? *You need to socialize more. Become involved with more people. Yes, it's nice that you do so much thinking in here, but you need to get out of your own head into the minds of others.* So, I did. I became more social. As a result of becoming more social, I came to recognize their beingness, their self-awareness, their intentionality. Trees are like people. And people are also like trees. We are not that separate. We are in relationship to each other. In a good human relationship, we recognize the separate existence of the other, the personhood of the other. We respect and may revere the other. We are together in a reciprocal relationship. The trees wanted that from me.

TWO WOMEN

Several women came with me to visit the King and the Queen. Two encounters were particularly remarkable. You have already met Amalia and Diane earlier in the Charlottesville chapter.

AMALIA

Amalia, who communicated with trees more than I did, rushed down the slope in bare feet to the base of the King and hugged him for more than an hour. She did not want to leave him. She said she learned so much from him. I began singing "Earth Angel," a song it turned out that her father liked to sing, to get her to come back so we could get going.

On later forest hikes, a giant image of Amalia appeared to be playing hide and seek with me, disappearing behind a tree and then reappearing. After I told her about this image of her, she told me that in another forest she played hide and seek, disappearing behind a tree then popping out with the children for whom she was a camp counselor. When I told her what I had seen of her, she said that she had seen me sitting cross-legged, floating above the trees with a big smile on my face.

She was having trouble graduating from the University of Virginia. The King and Queen told me to introduce her to Juliet, who later helped me start The Coincidence Project. The trees told me to make the introduction before October 31, 2016. I did as they requested. Amalia and Juliet immediately liked each other. Juliet guided her through the requirements for graduation. Juliet has become Amalia's spirit mother. The timeliness of their introduction to each other seemed to be known by the trees since Juliet, unknowingly, was about to lose her second parent soon after October 31. Amalia helped fill the subsequent family void.

DIANE

Remember my coincidental meeting with Diane on my way into the woods at Mint Springs, as described earlier in chapter 17?

After we met that day, we trekked up the mountain eventually coming to the King and Queen. I asked Diane to pause about fifteen feet from the place I usually stood looking directly at them from the path. I connected with them, told them Diane was here, and other things. Then I waved Diane to come stand next to me so that I could introduce her to them. As I was about to introduce her to the Queen, I saw Diane and the Queen interacting already as if they were quite familiar with each other. They were really into each other. "I guess you don't need an introduction," I mumbled. Then Diane shooed me away so she could commune with the Queen more privately. When she waved me back, I suggested she form a rhombus with the triad. "I already did," she said. My face scrunched again in surprise and disbelief. Diane has been and is tuned in to the Divine Feminine, which radiates from the Queen.

INTERACTING WITH THE THREES

I had been communing with the King and Queen for about eight years, when I noticed another tree standing halfway between them (from where I stood up on the trail) and about twelve feet behind them. The third tree was about the same height although lower down into the little valley through which the creek that nourished them flowed. How did I not see it? Was it their child? Was it male or female? I concluded it was a She/Him and as the current fashion suggested, I could call the third tree "Z." Sometimes I thought Z was the brains behind the outfit, but who knows.

I love to sing in the forest, mostly romance songs from the 1950s. The King and the Queen and Z like me to sing to them. How do I know? They seem to smile by emanating pleasurable energy that bounces between us. Sometimes I go up there with no interest in singing and then standing there in front of them, they ask for a song. A few forest hikers know me as the man who sings to trees. Why do the trees like me to sing to them? My Danish anthropologist friend Julie Mariel said, "They like you singing to them because they do not have voices to create that vibration. You do. And they help you as best as they can with the vibration frequency they have."

Some of the songs they seem to like are geo-romantic; they include mountains and sky. The especially like "The Morning Side of the Mountain" and "Over the Rainbow."[3]

---

3. Tommy Edwards sang "The Morning Side of the Mountain" in 1958, and Judy Garland sang "Over the Rainbow," in The Wizard of Oz in 1939.

A verse from each song is:

The Morning Side of the Mountain

There was a girl, there was a boy
If they had met they might have found a world of joy
But she lived on the morning side of the mountain
And he lived on the twilight side of the hill

Over the Rainbow

Somewhere over the rainbow
Way up high
There's a land that I heard of
Once in a lullaby

One piece of their advice was both helpful and harmful to me. As I mentioned earlier, I was having major trouble with the copyright of my radio program. The producer owned *my* radio show because the law says that the person who puts the ideas into material form owns the material form, and therefore the content on it. The trees told me to give him an ultimatum. I did. I never got the copyright, but my blood pressure went way up, so I had to increase my medication dosage. It made for a clear break from that producer, which turned out to be a very good move.

What is the benefit of talking with trees? To believe that trees are conscious beings like dogs and cats shatters dearly held modern scientific beliefs. This practice helps to open human beings up to conversations with other life-forms, guardian angels, the ECCO (Earth Coincidence Control Center), or perhaps intergalactic agents. These others remain hypothetical to me but not to some other people I know. As Shakespeare's Hamlet said, "There are more things in heaven and earth, Horatio, / Than are dreamt of in your philosophy."

And so, I asked the "Threes" if they were conduits for communications from beyond the psychosphere, from beyond Earth's mental and physical atmosphere. At that moment they appeared to be antennae, capable of transmitting information through them to me. "Who are you?" I asked. *You wouldn't be able to comprehend. Since you need a name, call us Pleiadians.* That label was convenient because I had recently interviewed on my podcast, a woman who had been told when she was about three that she was from Pleiades. It took years for her to match the childhood name with the star system we call Pleiades.

Where I stood with the Threes created a rhombus, a four-sided parallelogram with sides of equal length whose angles, unlike a square, were not at 90 degrees to each other. We became a three-dimensional One, which appeared to possibly be a portal into another consciousness. Creating this geometric shape from their triangle moved me to dance with them, to do the rhombus. I moved my hands up and down, paralleling the trunks of the King and the Queen. My left hand moved up and down with the Queen's trunk. My right hand moved up and down with the King's trunk. And my body vibrated with Z who was directly in front of me behind the other two. In a trance I became more treelike, their treeness entered into my being, the feeling of bark, of wood, of strength, and their essence in me . . . in me. With a slow polite letting go, I re-emerged into everyday consciousness feeling much more a part of the forest and feeling a deeper connection with the trees, not just the Threes but each tree that I met afterward, especially those surrounding my house.

A few weeks later, we were discussing the rhombus and the possibility of a pentagon by including someone with whom the Threes had already established a connection. They made it clear, more by feeling than by words, that there had to be a strong connection between me and the other person so that the pentagram would be stable. I once had a strong connection with Amalia, who had connected deeply with the King years before, but when we headed up there Amalia ran out of steam due to Lyme disease. The connection between Diane and me had become wobbly. So, no one joined us.

The communications were becoming feel-thought rather than just feeling or just thought words. (It feels so good to be with them.) I translated these communications into practical language. This time they told me to let them remotely access me, the way troubleshooting computer technicians remotely access distressed laptops and desktops. So, I meta-phorically clicked on Okay, and they operated my body into dancing the rhombus with them at dance the next day. It was like having a vir-tual reality headset on but without the equipment.

With the Threes, I pretended to be a tree, or more accurately allowed myself to become a tree. Or tried to become a tree. I lined up with them, danced our dance, sometimes going low below ground as well as high to the treetops, imagining the roots of each tree being connected in a large underground matted fungus-root mind, feeding, communicating along massively long fiber networks among the trees. Imagining running my mind along their matted mind climbing roots into other trees, feeling them feeling me, maybe knowing me, maybe knowing them.

SPECULATION ON TREE-ME TELEPATHY

I began to believe that they do not necessarily think in English. What they do is find the words and sentences available in my vocabulary and syntax, organize them in ways that I can understand, and then release them into my consciousness. In this way, the communication gives the appearance of telepathy.

LOVELY LITTLE SMALL THINGS

Lovely little small things happened with the trees and me. A few yards from my usual place to stand in front of the King and Queen, I was cry-ing joyfully while watching a video on my phone of my grandson Max, about four years old. Max really liked Batman and had some booklets and Legos of his hero. It was not lost on him that his last name is Beitman so that if you replace the *ei* with an *a* you get Max Batman. I looked up from crying. A family of five was coming toward me and the last one was a boy about Max's age with a Batman shirt. I said, "Hi Batman."

At another time, I was singing a romantic song to the three trees. As I was finishing the song, I stretched my arms out to each side in a grand eloquent ending gesture. As I stretched my arms and hands out, a fall-ing leaf gently touched my right hand on the way down. I was touched!

The communications continue.

PART 2

Serial Coincidences

Part 2 illustrates the serial coincidences available across our lifespans. These series highlight our personal patterns and our challenges. To see them requires knowing they exist. Knowing they exist illuminates obscure life patterns that can be more consciously acknowledged and managed. Not only is it true for large groups but also for individuals— "those who cannot remember the past are condemned to repeat it." Awareness of pattern repetition over many years can spark curiosity about how each personal psyche creates and utilizes these lifelong patterns, and where possible, be more able to change the maladaptive ones.

Strings of observable things create serial coincidences. Each of the incidents in the series is observable by someone else, unlike those meaningful coincidences that involve a private mental event. I can't peer into your mind to see an image you are remembering or experiencing that matches an external event that I could see. Your skull, your brain, and your mind are opaque to me. Only you know. But I can possibly verify stories of two or more observables in the external world that make up strings of recurrent things.

Over my lifetime, I have been part of several different emotionally charged serial coincidences. The first involved a teammate on my high school football and baseball teams. The second involved my relationships with human hearts, including my own. The third describes several close calls, physical near-death experiences.

20
That Tom

FOUR TIMES WHILE I WAS RUNNING for a sure touchdown, a team-mate stopped me from scoring.

JEALOUSY KNOCKS ME DOWN

My senior year in high school (1959–60) our football team went unde-feated 9–0, we won the conference title, and I was selected for the All-Conference team. In two of those games, the right offensive tackle and longtime teammate, Tom Paton, made well-intentioned moves that disrupted two of my long touchdown runs. In a close game against P. S. Dupont, I pulled away downfield with only the goal line in front of me. While on my toes, in high gear, Tom ran into me, knocking me down. Supposedly he was looking for someone to block, but no one was near me.

While playing against A. I. Dupont, I was returning a punt behind a wall of blockers aligned along the side lines. . . Tom said to Frank, one of the guards positioned next to him in the wall, about an opponent running at me, "You get this guy low and I'll get him high." To do that, one or both of them stepped back into the alley forcing me to swerve and step out of bounds. I did not realize I had stepped out of bounds. As I was trotting to the goal line, the whistle blew. The run was called back. Again, no touchdown. Okay, wasn't that enough, Tom, stopping me on two touchdown runs?

I would have had six touchdowns that year and matched Joe Biden's number of TDs. He played at Archmere Academy, a school down the road from my high school.

Playing for Swarthmore College, I broke into the open against Ursinus on their home turf. Downfield about twenty-five yards our left end, Bill Jewett bumped into me. There was no one for him to block. I was running high on my toes, a careful balance to increase speed. I tipped over and hit the ground. No score.

Then Bill Jewett got best athlete award for the senior class. I asked the assistant dean of students what happened, how that was decided: "You got enough press," he said. "Time to give someone else deserved recognition."

Against Johns Hopkins, I was again in the open with only the goal posts in front of me. Maybe ten to fifteen yards away from me, our right halfback clipped one their players (an illegal block). That player had no chance of catching me. Once again, no touchdown when there looked like open space between the goal line and me.

📝 Doctor's Notes

To determine the probabilities of these physical coincidences involves estimating the number of times a teammate interferes with a running back who is in the clear running for a touchdown as a percentage of the total number of long touchdown runs that a ball carrier makes. The unnecessary illegal block happens more often than knocking down a teammate in the open; thus it is the higher probability event, so we can leave it out of the estimate. My subjective probability (my sense of the likelihood) lowered the probability because it *happened to me three times*! Why? My teammates were playing the game as they thought they should and yet they stopped me. In only one instance did their stopping me change the outcome. Against Ursinus in 1962 we lost 8–14.

How to explain a teammate disrupting my path to score? My guess is that their motivation was out of their awareness. On the football team, Tom played offensive and defensive tackle—the grunt work on a football team. Our high school coach advised us running backs to "take the tackles out for a milkshake" since they get none of the recognition that we star power backfield guys did. I learned this lesson really clearly fifty years later while telling a good friend, a psychologist, about some of my football days. He had also played in the line in tough, brutal combat. Finally, he had heard enough and slugged me in the shoulder. I stopped. "You got the glory, Bernie," he declared. Maybe my teammates were jealous of my ability to make touchdowns. Our subconscious operates on the football field, too.

Tom Got Me Again

Tom and I played a lot of baseball together: two years in the Babe Ruth League (ages 13–15), two years on American Legion (ages 16–18), and two years on the high school baseball team.

In the spring of our senior year on the baseball diamond, I had hits for each of the first five times at bat, continuing the hot hitting of the previous spring when I won the conference batting title. As I hit a little flare that landed over the shortstop's head, Tom, from the bench for everyone to hear, loudly moaned something like, "Oh, not again. Beitman is just lucky." After that, my batting average tanked. The groove, the flow, the being in the present, was replaced by being too self-aware. Tom had jinxed me.

🗒 Doctor's Notes

Ian Fleming, the creator of James Bond, wrote in *Goldfinger*: "Mr. Bond, they have a saying in Chicago: 'Once is happenstance. Twice is coincidence. The third time it's enemy action.'" Does this idea apply here to Tom?

Tom was a stalwart teammate. We respected each other. Human beings are full of contradictions. Sometimes we need to weigh the good against the difficulties in someone close to us.

Ideally I should take these undercutting instances as compliments. By writing them down and making this comment, I am making a big step toward doing just that.

As I review this section, I am dealing with a guy at dance who is competitive with me. These reminders of how teammates can undercut me when I am succeeding, encourage me to protect myself from this person's negative impact on me.

Principle

Jealousy, competitiveness, and undercutting are unfortunately part of the behavior of humans in groups. Even if your team is unified in its goal directedness, be alert to those who might wish to undercut you. If you are outstanding in some way, the potential for jealous acts against you increase.

21
Heart Trouble

I GOT WRAPPED UP in heart trouble in multiple ways.

You Gotta Have Heart

Tenth grade. My mother wouldn't sign the permission slip for me to play football, so I missed all the Junior Varsity games in ninth grade. Finally, my father did. The team was bussed to a camp somewhere, maybe Pennsylvania, maybe New Jersey, but not in our little state of Delaware. The temperature was in the nineties with high humidity, and we were wearing full pads (shoulder, hips, and helmet) and running around a half-mile field with the baseball backstop the only area with a little shade. The coaches stood at the four corners making sure we didn't cut those corners. I was panting, my dark green shirt soaked in sweat. "Keep moving! You can do it!" I began to have my doubts. Pushing ahead. Straining. Two laps. Three laps. Was it seven we had to do? Losing count. Stumbling toward the next corner coach. Rounding onto the baseball field through left field, grinding toward third base and the little bit of shade behind the backstop, my heart began to talk to me. I imagined the headline in what we called the Wilmington garbage wrapper (some people did wrap their garbage in newspaper then): "Mt. Pleasant High School sophomore football player dies of heart attack while running in full pads in hot humidity." That headline played over and over in my dehydrated, exhausted, languidly stumbling mind.

Football practice was never as hard again. That hot summer heat run had toughened me up, helped me see I could endure adversity by perseverance, and probably set the stage for my classmates' success our senior year when we went undefeated.

A Nerve Is Like a Muscle

As twenty-two-year-old medical students, we had to choose a specialty. I had narrowed my choice down to being either a cardiologist or psychiatrist. Because the heart seemed to be just a pump, cardiology did not seem that interesting to me, so I drifted toward psychiatry.

During the first year, each medical student was obligated to thoroughly bore our classmates during two three-hour sessions in which we each presented fifteen minutes of something about microanatomy—looking at cells of the body through a microscope. I wanted to liven things up a bit. I decided to present slides of the Purkinje fibers of the heart, which conduct electrical impulses that coordinate its rhythmic beating. These were muscle cells that had evolved to act like nerves—brain-like activity in the heart. Cardiological psychiatry?

I was scheduled to present about halfway through the three hours the day before Thanksgiving vacation. We all wanted to get out of there.

Creatively ensconced in the Yale Medical School historical library (wooden panels, old books, musty smell), I composed a song for the occasion.

When my time came, I strode from the back of the classroom to the front, guitar held high above my head like the Beatles entering Madison Square Garden. I showed slides of heart muscle cells and Purkinje fiber cells and remarked on the evolution of Purkinje fibers evolving from primitive hearts. Then I picked up the guitar and started singing and chordlessly strumming this song.

> *My Daddy he once told me*
> *Oh, so long ago,*
> *A nerve is like a muscle, son*
> *This I feel you should know.*

I looked at him
And cried, amazed
Why Daddy, what do you mean?
One moves, the other moves it.
The similarity can't be seen.

The third verse is lost to posterity.

Some of my classmates silently howled and a few looked anxiously back to the two professors in the back of the room.

On the way out, the senior professor stopped me to report, "That was the worst presentation I have ever heard." But he could not fail me; Yale Medical School did not give out grades. We only had to pass Parts 1 and 2 of the National Boards to graduate.

Soon afterward, I was summoned to the dean's office to meet with the acting dean of students. He described the scene. "Did you do that?"

"Yes, I did."

He had the conventional Harvard (but this was Yale) wire-rimmed glasses and bow tie and tried to stifle a laugh. He was only partially successful. "Don't do it again."

"Okay," I said and left.

Postscript: One spring Saturday afternoon about a year later, the junior professor attending that presentation was standing along the sidelines of a Yale rugby match. During our labs, he made it clear that he did not think much of me. I was playing wing, the closest player to the fans. I paused, waiting to see which way the ball was going to go. I heard a voice nearby. "What are you doing here?" I turned to see the bewildered junior professor.

"I didn't have anything else to do," I said. That got him. I ran off and never saw him again. I imagined his thinking, "How could that stupid nerd of a student be playing first team for Yale rugby?"

The meaning of many coincidences is in the moment they occur. Sometimes that meaning is a good laugh, a smile, happiness, joy, a touch of wonder. And a fond memory. I so enjoyed his annoyed surprise.

THE TELLTALE HEART

Peter O, a bulky man in his fifties, could not walk for more than a few yards down the hospital hall on the surgical floor without labored breathing. His cough contained blood. As we walked, he told me, "I can't live like this." As my first real patient in the third-year clinical rotations, I was to be present with him while he was on the cardiac surgeon's operating table.

Encircled by the tubes of the primitively massive heart-lung machine filled with flowing blood, I stood at his left knee. With his chest sawed open through his sternum, Peter had been hooked up to the breathing, pumping, heart-replacing machine while the surgeon entered his heart to replace his calcified aortic valve. The surgeon chipped away at the rock-hard calcium around his valve, then lowered the birdcage-shaped replacement, sewed it in, and let blood flow back into his heart to see if the new valve held.

It did not hold. Blood spurted around the seated valve. The tiny mounds of calcifications prevented the new valve from seating tightly on the absent but necessary pliable flesh. The blood squirted through the tiny valleys between the calcified mounds. I plaintively asked, "Is this going to work?" Imagine the scowls of the two surgeons in response. Fifty pints of blood later, they gave up. Peter could no longer live.

That scene is vividly scorched in my memory.

Psychiatry started looking even more appealing.

RENAL ARTERY BALLOON

During my psychiatric residency, I was urgently called home to Wilmington, Delaware; my father was to undergo a laparotomy because he had a pulsing mass in his abdomen. A CT scan was not available in the early 1970s. They had to cut him open to see what was going on. Very Primitive! Because I was an M.D., I was allowed to scrub into the operation. The old surgeon stuck a 25-gauge (very thin) needle into the pulsing mass. (All he had to do was feel the thing pulsing to know it was a ballooning artery!) Blood dribbled out that would not stop. The continued bleeding required an emergency helicopter lift to Philadelphia where they cut out the weakened hepatic (liver) artery and sewed in a graft for the ballooned-out section of the vessel wall. To make matters worse, after the graft was in place, his kidneys were not receiving enough blood because they had re-laid the blood vessels incorrectly. The surgeons had to open him up (now for the third time) to correctly place his arteries and veins. That was enough already!

Little did they know but the artificial graft had a fungus that then slowly spread through his body, weakened his esophageal arteries, and deteriorated his health. A year later this sixty-four-year-old man had shrunken in size and now looked twenty years older. I remember seeing the delight in his eyes when he saw me on my return home to see him. He would end up choking on his own blood on my thirty-first birthday. Three thousand miles away, at around the same time, I was standing over a sink uncontrollably choking myself. As described earlier, seeded by that experience, I invented the term *simulpathity*—feeling the pain of a loved one at a distance. Each time I tell this story, I honor the memory of Karl Beitman.

The deaths of Peter O. and my father have fed a strong distrust of physicians even as I am a bona fide member of the guild.

HEARTY ROAD TO ACADEMIC SUCCESS

When I left my faculty job in Seattle, a seed was planted for my long simmering psychiatric romance with cardiology. Described earlier in more detail, knocking on the door of colleague Wayne Katon led to a career-enhancing research idea—studying when chest pain is more likely panic disorder than heart disease. The chest pain of some panic attacks can be confused with the terror of a heart attack. Ironically, the more symptoms you have, the less likely you are to be having a heart attack. If you are under forty and female with multiple symptoms (shortness of breath, nausea or abdominal distress, numbness and tingling, fear of losing control) there is not much to worry about cardiologically. Yes, psychiatrically!

My forty papers on the subject seem to still be the most anyone has written on the topic.

REJECTION TRIGGERS HIGH BLOOD PRESSURE
AND ATRIAL FIBRILLATION

An impossible romance triggered my hypertensive crisis when the woman I was seeing suddenly declared her intention to reunite with her high school boyfriend. With a blood pressure reading of 250/110 (normal 120/80), I knew I was in trouble, called an ambulance, and enjoyed the experience of being rattled off in that bouncy vehicle to the Emergency Department as a real crisis patient. I stayed overnight. They did nothing but watch me. I felt like an anthropologist visiting a nearby territory that I'd never experienced—doctor as ER patient.

I serendipitously got a rapid outpatient appointment (a time had opened up unexpectedly) and cruised in to see Dr. R at the University of Virginia outpatient cardiology clinic. Dr. R quickly helped subdue the hypertensive crisis, achieving the needed systolic drop from 200 to 125. Relief!

But that was not enough heartache for me.

Another woman had been the source of yet more emotional difficulty. I was trying to learn my lesson. So I told her by text to stop contacting me. The anger and hurt that permeated her text message response triggered my physically and emotionally vulnerable heart into atrial fibrillation. I was recovering from intense radiation for my prostate cancer and should not have gone to dance the day before and should not have gone to work where I received the anger-laden text. I was exhausted.

My first awareness of a heart problem came two days later on the elliptical machine at the gym when I became short of breath and couldn't do my usual routine. Maggie, the compassionate, friendly nurse practitioner read my EKG and pronounced: Afib (atrial fibrillation). The atria of my heart were beating too fast, not allowing adequate blood flow to my body. In came the interventional cardiologist who wanted to insert a device that would reduce the likelihood of stroke from Afib. Having been on the other side of that relationship, I knew she was looking for business with her super friendly reassuring manner. She was selling her wares. Strokes usually create enormous disability (inability to walk, talk, and move arms in the worst situations).

Doctors are trained to imagine the worst, indirectly passing on their fears to their patients. Fear makes for more business. I declined the device to wait to see what happens to the Afib. I wanted to see if taking care of myself might make a difference.

Dr. R prescribed blood thinners to reduce the risk from 3 percent to 1 percent, which meant that if I cut myself, I might be in trouble since the blood thinners decrease clotting and increase bleeding time. These molecules also increase the likelihood of brain bleeds.

After the five-day episode, I had three more episodes over the next eighteen months, each lasting fewer than five hours, which were quelled by intense walking. Since that fourth one in 2019, there have been none. I hope it stays that way!

Meanwhile, as I was seeing what careful, healthy living might do, then came scare number two. My heart rate can be under 50, sometimes 43. That's supposedly bad. Dr. R shuffled me over to an 8:00 AM Monday morning consultation with another interventional cardiologist who kindly offered to put a pacemaker in my heart to speed it up to 70 beats per minute. The nurse took my blood pressure. Systolic 190! Oh, this again. Listening to my body screaming, I refused the pacemaker. Soon afterwards, my blood pressure came back into the normal range.

HEARTFELT COMMENTS

So my cardiologist misadventures continued. First was Peter's tragic aortic valve replacement, then my father's surgeon putting a needle in his throbbing hepatic artery, and finally Dr. R scaring me into hypertension. No wonder many people do not trust the medical profession. The primary injunction to physicians is, First, do no harm. These physicians did not get the message. Only Peter's cardiac surgeon seemed to have no alternative but to operate. My father's surgeon and Dr. R failed in their obligation to do no harm, although each had thought he was helping. They were wrong.

What does this series of heart-focused issues say to me about me?

Mortality: At age sixteen running around the half-mile field in ninety-degree high humidity with full pads on, I glimpsed myself as deceased from a heart attack.

The heart has brain-like qualities: As a first-year medical student, I learned that all is not what it appears to be. What I thought was a purely muscular pump had evolved some of its cells to conduct electrical activity that gave that pump its much-needed coordination. For the optimal function of the whole, some cells learned to hold synaptic hands to pass along electrical messages essential to the functioning of the entire organ. All this electrical activity in the heart creates a magnetic field much stronger than the magnetic field created by the brain's electrical activity. The heart's magnetic field contains information and energy that can be sensed by others in the vicinity. That information and energy often takes the form of emotion. The heart then is our emotional brain, as poets and songwriters and all those of us who are caught in the throes of romantic love and broken hearts know so well.

Surgeons have limits: As a naive third-year medical student, I thought surgeons were all powerful. No! Allopathic medicine, that Western form of treatment that sees the body only as a machine, has many limitations. Though it has its place, allopathic medicine is too often interested in making money and too often controlled by drug companies and device makers. Nutritional advice is sadly lacking in the medical "armamentarium," which sees its functions as a war against disease. Disease can be a message of hope about how to change yourself. Psycho-spiritual dimensions can be fostered in medical care with attention to synchronicity.

When that surgeon put a 25-gauge needle into my father's aneurysm, the streak of destructiveness and stupidity in physicians became glaringly obvious. And the well-intentioned suggestion by my cardiologist that resulted in a huge blood pressure surge continued to make it yet more obvious that all of us should discern for which problems Western medicine is useful, and when to look elsewhere.

And the lesson from research showing that anxiety triggers symptoms resembling heart attacks: more evidence that the brain and the heart, the mind and the emotional heart, are closely related.

One of our most surprising findings was that some people go to cardiac catheterization with standard heart attack symptoms but they are not frightened or do not express anxiety. They have no heart disease and fit panic disorder criteria. We called this the non-fear panic disorder. What?! Isn't that a contradiction? Life on this planet is filled with opposites.

HEARTBREAK CAN BE PHYSIOLOGICALLY REAL!

Two impossible relationships led to damaging my heart and its vascular system. These were dramatic lessons for me. A year or so later, the first heartbreaker asked me to dinner, had a strong drink, and asked to live with me. I was in love with the soon-to-trigger atrial fibrillation person, so I fortunately declined what would have been a terribly tumultuous relationship. The blood pressure crisis was a small price to pay for what could have been romantic disaster.

Informed by my distrust of allopathic medicine, I set about trying to heal myself. The blood pressure problem has been helped by pharmaceutical medication and yoga. I treated the atrial fibrillation by trying to take better care of myself, which included avoiding potentially traumatic rejections while also learning how not to be terrified of being hurt in a relationship with a woman.

I've loved being in love most of my life, probably beginning with my infant romance with my mother. I like to sing romantic songs from the 1950s. I hope I am learning how to love and be loved rather than being in love.

Doctor's Notes

Listen to your heart can be sage advice. When talking about intuitive knowing, we include potential information from the heart as well as the still, small voice in our minds and gut feelings.

I've been "listening" more closely. The heart information comes into my consciousness as different tone-feelings. Situations press specific feeling-tones in my heart like piano keys. I have been able to detect and locate feeling-tones of jealousy, yearning, rescuing, anger, and guilt. Labeling the feeling-tone helps to manage it. While I am talking with someone, my heart sends an overall feeling of pressure to my awareness. I've learned to interpret this pressure as "you've talked enough. Time to stop."

As the colors of the rainbow make up the fullness of light, the feeling-tones of the heart summate into the grand emotions of love and hate. The state of indifference seems to have the heart in neutral, no keys being pressed.

─────── **Principle** ───────

The heart generates emotional information that can be registered by others nearby.

─────────────────────────

According to the HeartMath Institute, the heart is the most powerful source of electromagnetic energy in the human body. The heart's electrical field is about sixty times greater in amplitude than the electrical activity generated by the brain. Furthermore, the magnetic field produced by the heart is more than a hundred times greater in strength than the field generated by the brain and can be detected up to three feet away from the body, in all directions. This field carries emotional information that can be registered in the brains of people open to such communications.[1]

More than the brain, the heart appears to be the source of our strongest emotions. Attending to the emanations from your heart can increase your ability to emotionally communicate with others. And your attunement to the heart energy of the other person can help you understand how that person feels about you.

Love. What is love? Why is the heart so prominent in depictions of love? If you have not loved someone you may know the feeling from songs and poetry. How can I let you know the feeling I have when the woman I love smiles, when she laughs, when she is happy? My heart

─────────────────────────

1. *Science of the Heart*, ebook available on the HeartMath Institute website.

expands and then I can't find the words. I can describe the welling of joyful tears.

And Divine Love. I have felt it. So hard to describe. Heart exploding joyfully, painfully, joyfully, so hard to contain the feeling in my chest. The feeling is there. Words fail me.

22
Close Calls

COMING TO THE EDGE OF A CLIFF when there is a strong wind behind you can be scary. How do you get out of that situation? Get low and wait for the wind to subside? Why did you go out on that cliff so close to the edge? What were you thinking?

Here are four instances of my being near that edge of a steep cliff with a howling wind at my back. Writing this book is evidence I survived.

THE BRIDGE TO NOWHERE

I had been tackled on the Swarthmore football field. I was in an awkward position with my head and feet on the ground but not the rest of my body. My body was like a bridge. The other team kept piling on. We had practiced this so my neck was strong enough to hold their weight. Finally, they got off. And no one knew I could have broken my neck.

📝 Doctor's Notes

My mother only came to the last game of my football career. She had this idea that football was a dangerous sport—all those other guys, bigger than I was, trying to hit me. The newspaper description of me as an All-Conference halfback included, "He's the smartest runner in the conference." I could fake, juke, and change directions, as well as sprint into openings. I didn't mind getting hit and I liked running into bigger guys if they were between me and the goal line.

But my mother was right. I could have been severely injured. Luckily, I relaxed and held my position until the pile collapsed.

A year later during my junior year, I took a part-time job taking care of a guy about my age who had broken his neck on a trampoline. His legs didn't work, his arms trembled. He had some control of his hands and arms. I'd pick him up, put him in his wheelchair, and help him eat. He represented one of my worst fears: not being able to run. He could see the baseball field from his bedroom window. He was a prisoner in his own body. That could have been me.

AUTOMATIC BRAIN SAVES A LIFE

In San Francisco, as I was driving away from the marijuana-dealing house, the Yellow Submarine, a child ran in front of my 1968 Volvo. My foot slammed on the brake *and only then did I see the child*. I had nearly killed someone. My brain had short-circuited my conscious awareness to trigger my leg and foot into action. It was like touching a hot stove and pulling away quickly and then realizing the stove was hot. But there is nothing magical here. The brain is wired for fast nonconscious deliberate action. Whew!

📝 Doctor's Notes

This bypassing conscious intention through activating ancient brain circuits had probably been exercised by running scared with the football. My senior year at Swarthmore, I was running back a punt. Without thinking about what I was doing, I eluded five tacklers. As the sixth one approached, I started to realize I had dodged five would-be tacklers. At that moment of direct conscious awareness, I got slammed. I had lost touch with the automatic circuits. Becoming aware of myself got me out of the flow.

Principle

A key brain circuit enables us to bypass rational thought to spring us to action. Your amygdala is a central player.

THE CURVE TO NOWHERE

While living in Redwood City on the Peninsula south of San Francisco and north of Palo Alto, the quarterback for my Swarthmore football team introduced me to a guy with a motorcycle who lived on Skyline Drive. The two-lane curvy road traveled along the tops of the small mountain range between the Pacific Ocean and the San Francisco Bay. I rode up to his place on my recently purchased BSA 500 bored out to 650, which meant that the cylinders driving the engines had increased volume so they could burn more gas per stroke, speeding up the power and acceleration. It's cute little tank was green, speckled with gold. I loved to watch my image on the bike reflected in the store windows on business Route 1, El Camino Real.

Somehow I ended up chasing this guy on Skyline Drive heading north. This curvy road was well-known to him but not to me. His motorcycle was quick and so was my BSA. He disappeared around a curve. Trying to catch up to him, I swerved into the other lane. A car going the opposite direction was suddenly right in front of me. As I squeezed over to my lane without tipping, I watched my left handlebar come within a few inches of the car door. I was wearing only a bicycle helmet. I meandered down to my house in Redwood City and quickly sold the bike. That was a near-death experience of the in-the-real-world kind.

📝 Doctor's Notes

I had owned motorcycles before. The first was 90cc and the second was 150cc, each much less powerful than the BSA 650cc. I had never raced before and did not know the territory. I had jumped into the unknown and almost crashed.

Principle

To increase synchronicities often relies on taking a chance on chance. Taking chances requires being alert in the moment to avoid disaster. This race was a stupid chance to take. A minor good outcome was possible. Bad outcomes were more likely.

RIPTIDE

On our honeymoon at the Sandpiper Inn on the shores of the Olympic Peninsula, I waded into the calm Pacific Ocean. The water was slowly ebbing toward the shore so I could wade deeper and deeper. Suddenly, it was as if the plug had been pulled and all that slow-moving water was now rushing past me. I put my shoulder to the pressure and planted my feet as if some lineman were trying to push me. My luck was having not gone so deep that I could keep my head and shoulders above water and dig my feet into the sandy bottom. After the water had all rushed out, I looked down at the pit in the sand my resistance had created. Pretty deep. I was close to being washed out to sea by a riptide.

Doctor's Notes

Love of the ocean and not knowing about riptides led to the experience of being almost washed out to sea. Was it also a comment on the marriage I was entering? I think so. I loved the idea of love and marriage, but the undercurrents were dangerous and unknown.

Principle

Fools rush in where angels fear to tread. Maybe because the angels know better. Look before you leap. These are time-tested aphorisms worth keeping in mind.

OVERALL COMMENT

Four examples of putting myself in risky situations. I've taken many other chances without tragedy grasping me. Each of us has to be careful about attributing being saved to divine intervention and from that to conclude that our life was saved to carry out an important mission here on Earth. So many people have died before accomplishing what they thought was their life mission. I'm glad I am around to write these stories.

━━━━━━━━━━━━━━━━━ **Overall Principle** ━━━━━━━━━━━━━━━━━

Be grateful when you survive near-death events and continue to carry out what you have discovered to be your purpose in life. You will have to take a chance on chance but not too chancy. The motorcycle race is an example of a foolish chance to take. Try to remember to weigh the cost and weigh the benefit.

━━

Synchronicity Shows Us How We Are Interconnected

OUR WORLD IS SPINNING into collective madness. Human beings are the primary cause. I passionately believe that meaningful coincidences can help us mitigate the looming destruction by direct experiences of our interconnectedness. As we recognize the reality of our interdependence, we can master the many challenges confronting us.

EGO

Our Egos Need Careful Management

In these coincidence stories of my life you can see that I used many meaningful coincidences to make me feel better about myself, to give myself a sense of specialness. In writing this book, in writing this paragraph, I recognize my need to have a positive effect and be recognized for it. Can I let this drive, this need, dissipate into nothingness? Should I? Or as several of my friends suggest, should I just let my gifts flow through me?

A fact-based way to reduce synchronicity-induced self-aggrandizement is found in the recurrence of similar synchronicities across large swaths of humanity. *If it is happening to me, it has happened to others or will happen to others or could be happening to someone else right now.* Your experiences truly *are* amazing to you. Yet many other people are experiencing coincidences much like yours.

PERSONAL SYNCHRONICITY FACILITATORS
Pattern Recognition Can Help Free Us

Pattern repetition characterizes human behavior, thought, emotion, and imagination. Freud labeled this tendency *the repetition compulsion*. Jung described repetition through the recurrence of archetypes.

Much of nature involves pattern repetition. Just look around: the cycles of the seasons; the sun and the moon and their cycles; weather patterns; traffic patterns; the primary themes of fiction and history; as well as the patterns of your daily life. Pattern repetition characterizes our existence.

The pattern repetitions of meaningful coincidences alert us to examine what underlies them. Through the recognition of these repetitions, you can identify the underlying patterns of your synchronicity experiences to see how they can help you function and to individuate. They reflect your own ways of utilizing synchronicities. I knock on strangers' doors and swing from vine to vine in the coincidence jungle. Others may use dreams, voices, and deep intuition as their primary facilitators.

What are your synchronicity facilitating patterns? Appendix II lists ones that seem to be common to many people experiencing synchronicities. Find out by recording your stories and then reviewing them for patterns that create your coincidences. Perhaps AI could help define your patterns.

THE SYNCHRONICITY POLARITY
Everything Is Connected

Synchronicities challenge the conventional insistence that each of us is an island in the vast ocean of otherness. When your mind is reflected by events in your environment, you experience challenges to this belief in personal isolation and its commonly accompanying loneliness. With synchronicity experiences you will intuitively apprehend our collective human organism and our deep intertwining with the rest of the natural world. We too are part of nature. Plants and animals love playing synchronicity with humans.[1]

INDIVIDUATION

Evolve toward Your True, Authentic, Real Self

Jung urged people to individuate, to realize themselves to themselves. To individuate means becoming nondivided—a whole. Individuating people integrate the multiple aspects of themselves into their evolving wholeness by learning from experiences to become their increasingly unique selves.

Uniqueness is both shared by each of us and special to only you. Your individual uniqueness makes you different from all the other human beings on Earth because of that combination of traits and experiences that is ultimately only you. Your individuating uniqueness defines the limitations that provide you with a sense of existing. Your individuated uniqueness has within it your potential contributions toward mitigating the frightening trajectory we humans are creating.

Synchronicities accelerate individuation through experiencing the interconnectedness with all creatures on Earth with each other, including the living Earth itself. Each of us is an evolving individual, part of an evolving social context, part of the collective human organism, and part of the natural world. Your personal individuation can accelerate the individuation of the collective human organism.

Will others in your life also evolve or will you take separate paths? Or will some of those you love and like prefer to not change? Here lies some of the risk of personal individuation.

Individuation involves the ongoing incorporation of new discoveries, challenges, grief, loss, change, and success with a perpetual

---

1. Check out this YouTube video from Connecting with Coincidence, "Wild Animals Will Play With You!, Matthew Zylstra and Juliet Trail: EP 329," December 10, 2023.

learning about how to love and be loved, how to successfully move toward ideal relationships and to adapt to the ever-changing pressures of social and cultural and global changes. As you align your authenticity with the layers of interconnectedness of which you are a part, you continue individuating. You are both separate and part of layers of greater wholeness.

You continue to learn the limitations of your personal uniqueness. Embrace these limitations! They clarify the skills you have to make contributions toward improving life on this planet. You will likely find that synchronicity integrated with intuition becomes an increasingly more reliable guide as you flow between transcendence, your ego identity, and immanence—the experience of the oneness here on Earth.

NUMINOUS

Encounter the Transcendent

As you evolve your interconnectedness and personal uniqueness, you may experience numinous synchronicities that evoke a sense of the sacred, the divine, and the transcendent. You are being shown a glimpse of the potential vastness of your conscious experience. These events suggest that you may be experiencing the consciousness of the Earth or the psychosphere or beyond.

BEING DRAWN TO YOUR FUTURE

Allow Yourself to Evolve toward Your Personal Future

To what future are you personally being drawn?

Meaningful coincidences can offer guideposts, signposts, to suggest directions for you on your path into the future, waiting for you to grasp, ride, and evolve. It is not just about you becoming one with the Oneness. By spiritually bypassing earthly problems, people are avoiding the challenges of their personal life and the needs of the collective. By transcending to only spiritual experiences, they separate themselves from these realities. We are all in this together.

DISCERNMENT

Sharpen Ability to Judge through Trial and Error

The mechanics of finding the path to your role and continuing on it means paying attention to many key inputs. They include the several aspects of your intuitive knowing—gut feelings, heart urges, and the usually still, small voice coming through your mind (sometimes the voice gets pretty insistent). Watch for mind-mirrors, answers, and suggestions from your surroundings, including other people, numbers, signs, license plates, and various media including books, videos, and movies. Each of these requires carefully tuned judgments about usefulness or not, especially information from social media. In this polarized world, meaningful coincidences can be manufactured by others to take advantage of you as demonstrated by social media marketing.

The passage of time influences your perception of the positivity of a synchronicity. It may at first be good for one person and bad for another. Over time the judgment may be reversed (as I discuss in my book, *Meaningful Coincidences*). Positive effects from apparently awful coincidences may take months or years to become clear. Maintaining the belief that much is to be learned from the negative sharpens your ability to discern.

IMAGINATION

Exercise Your Imagination

The technological and social engineering of current world cultures try to rob you of your individual imagination, diverting it to consumerism and exciting distractions. To counter these vicious trends, take possession of your imagination. Together let's imagine the future we want, fighting off the lures and pressures of the technological and social norms.

Imagine what reality truly is. Imagine what can be real. The onslaught of media, news, and entertainment diverts our imagination into gutters of fear and isolation rather than to the heights of personal and collective ideals. As you find your role, your personal future, please try to consider how your role can accelerate positive transformation in your social group and for all of Earth.

YOUR CHOICE

You Have Free Will—You Have No Choice about That

Each of us has a range of freedom to choose. A percentage of humanity is not able or willing to notice our increasingly rapid movement toward collective self-harm. Another group inhibits the movement toward a positive evolution insisting that only their group members survive and flourish. Others see the suicidal trajectory and put their future in the hands of fate/God/Universe believing that they have no agency.

Each of us does decide, including those who decide to do nothing. Each of us is a cell in the collective human organism. Each of us affects the whole.

What do you choose to do?

Questions for Reflection

1. What is the Self Observer?

2. What does this mean to you: "What you are seeking is also seeking you."

3. How does your environment reflect what is going on in your mind?

4. Who has aided you in reaching goals you might not have reached without that person?

5. If you have a personally significant number, what is it and how does it help you?

6. How has the library angel or the internet angel helped you?

7. What do you think of divination methods like tarot cards and the I Ching?

8. How are psychosis and synchronicity related?

9. Have you experienced the pain/distress of a loved one who is somewhere else?

10. How have you experienced a major life stressor as a benefit?

APPENDIX II

Thought Patterns of Synchronicity Observers

THESE QUALITIES WERE DERIVED from the stories in this book using ChatGPT, based on the idea that each of our minds reflects aspects of our collective human mind.

1. Everything is connected: You believe that events and people are all connected in a meaningful way. Coincidences aren't just random—they have deeper significance.

2. Searching for proof of the mystical: You're often looking for evidence that mystical or spiritual experiences are real.

3. Feeling energy between people: You're sensitive to the energy exchanges between people and how these affect relationships.

4. Nature is alive and aware: You see nature as conscious beings that can communicate and have intentions.

5. Balancing two sides of yourself: You often deal with the challenge of balancing different parts of your identity—like being both mystical and scientific.

6. Finding meaning in hard times: When facing difficulties, you look for the lessons or deeper meanings in those experiences.

7. Being careful about personal boundaries: You're conscious of how others' energy can affect your own well-being and personal space.

8. Exploring how the mind works: You're fascinated by how consciousness, perception, and awareness shape our reality.

9. The past still matters: You often reflect on how past experiences continue to influence your present thoughts and actions.

10. Always curious: You have a strong curiosity and a desire to learn, especially about things that blur the line between what we know and the unknown.

11. Adapting and bouncing back: No matter the challenges, you show resilience and adapt to new situations.

Principles of Coincidence

THE FOLLOWING LIST WAS COMPILED from the coincidences in this book.

- The **loss of structure** opens up new possibilities—especially if you keep your eyes open to notice things, if you move around and follow the hints and clues and your own intuition. You can hunt for new ideas and adventures in the coincidence jungle.
- **Keep moving**, keep looking, especially in new places. You may unexpectedly find what you don't quite know you are seeking. Serendipities increase when you move through stimulus-rich environments.
- What you **expect to happen** increases the likelihood of that happening.
- We humans seem to have abilities that get us into places that demonstrate our interconnectedness and fulfill some of our needs. Learn to trust **your inner guidance system** by trial-and-error testing.
- Try **knocking** on a few rationally/intuitively selected doors!
- When expecting synchronicities that present you with eternal wisdom, guidance, support, or contact with Oneness, be careful. It could be the **trickster** at work, or maybe just a coincidence.
- Some **random** (statistically explainable) **coincidences can be remarkably fruitful**. Their subjective meaning is a neglected part of the probability estimate.
- The **natural world is singing** to us. Try tuning in.

- Our intuitions have access to immense stores of information in the psychosphere not readily available to our rational mind So **listen to your still, small voice, to your heart, to your gut**. Tune in and sharpen your understanding of their messages. Demanding situations can evoke unlikely solutions.

- During any window of time in which the **structure of daily life is loosened**, you have the option of following suggestions from your honed intuition.

- While many travel to foreign countries like India and Peru to gather new information to bring back home, new cultures can be found within Western countries from which to learn about the interrelatedness of all things.

- Having no coincidence (like police coming around the corner as Bill came out of the house) can also be more than pleasant.

- With evidence accumulating from mediums who can tell you things only you and your deceased loved one would know, to near-death experiences and evidence for reincarnation, perhaps you might consider, as I do, that **our minds/souls survive the death** of our bodies.

- Songs on the radio can demonstrate that our minds are more connected to our surroundings than Western cultures currently accept.

- **A culture that embraces synchronicities** is also likely to find that coincidences can help with social as well as personal transformation.

- **Take chances on chance** and maybe you will chance upon some chancy situations and some beautiful coincidences. Take a chance on chance.

- When you find yourself in the right place at the right time, **you may need to seize the moment** or the opportunity will drift away.

- A form of energy flows among and between people, especially on the dance floor. This energy can be amplified and diminished by our own actions. These energy movements may be less evident in nondance interactions. Awareness of interpersonal energy can be used positively and negatively. First **you have to believe it exists!**

- Meaningful coincidences often break the mold of dearly held conventional beliefs. Find ways to manage this ontological shock. If you are overwhelmed with synchronicities, you may need to **find a coincidence counselor** to help ground you. Talking with like-minded people is the best first step.
- Be open to the possibility that **patterns in your mind may sometimes be mirrored by the minds of others.** Be open to reflecting that mirror back on yourself.
- Intense **emotional connections** seem to linger, as is sometimes reflected by synchronicities.
- Meaningful coincidences **illuminate the invisible currents** that connect and unite us. Who will you coincidentally reconnect with from your brief intense past relationships? These re-encounters suggest that we are part of an invisible web that creates bonds through emotional intensity. The implications of continuing connections like these are profound for our disconnected humanity.
- One door closes and another door opens. Be sure to consider walking through the **next door.**
- What looks like a synchronicity may have a human cause.
- Coincidences can serve as markers for special memories.
- You may journey far and wide only to return to where you started.
- Each of us may have someone strikingly similar to us somewhere in the world. **Doppelgangers** ("double-goers" from German) are two strangers who share a remarkable number of characteristics; most commonly they look like identical twins. Fiction contains characters who are eerie mirror images of each other, such as in Charles Dickens's *A Tale of Two Cities.* The probability of a match depends on the characteristics you select. People may lead similar lives based on the complex interplay of cultural, social, and psychological factors that shape human experiences.
- **In the midst of a threat, remain calm**, listen to your intuition, and maybe a coincidence will ride to the rescue.
- We can **feel the pain of a loved one someplace else.** You have

to believe it is possible. Experiencing one dramatic instance can solidify the belief.

- **Imagining** helps to create the future. Make sure that what you imagine is what you really want, and that it is possible. Living in an igloo in Nome, Alaska, and imagining a man on a camel coming to sell you a rug is a highly unlikely possibility.
- The deceased sometimes seem to intervene in our lives.
- Sometimes we leave as we came.
- To **swing from vine to vine**, you have to be looking for the next vine and be willing to believe there will be another vine there and be ready to grab it.
- In addition to synchronicities, some **guides** for you will appear as human beings. Discern which ones to follow and which ones to let go. Keep learning which doors to knock on and then go strum your knuckles on that door.
- Hone your ability to recognize, listen to, and feel your **inner messaging**. These messages may come as a still, small voice, or an urge from your heart, or a gut feeling from the intricate nervous system of your intestines. Some of the messages from your inner messaging service may be wrong for the current circumstances. Learn to discriminate the useful ones from neutral ones and especially those leading to negative outcomes. One source of problems for most of us is negative self-talk—judgmental criticism of what we are doing. However, some of that negative self-talk may prove to be a useful course correction for you. Again, learn to discern your inner guides. **Learn to discern!**
- There are lots of jokers in this Earth life. The best you can do is laugh and learn.
- In the face of disappointment or loss, keep your eyes open for new possibilities rather than letting your head drop in sadness. **A drooping head** is unlikely to see openings, possibilities, and opportunities.
- To not grasp the opportunity violates your optimal path through life. Grasping creates the coincidence.

- Cast your net into uncertainty. You might find that what you are seeking is also seeking you.
- Weird coincidences happen. Their influence can be hard to judge.
- Sometimes getting what you want is a two-edged sword. In this polarized world, the **good and the bad often ride together**.
- The repercussions of your actions may benefit others. How many of those impacts do we never learn about?
- May you experience the loveliness of a closing synchronicity circle!
- Meaningful coincidences can provide **clues to how reality works**, including existential questions like why we are here and what happens after the body dies.
- Sometimes coincidences are to be enjoyed in the moment—funny, numinous (mystical), artistic, enthralling, inspiring, and worthy of a stand-up comedian.
- I wonder how often reciprocal needs could be met if people gave voice to them.
- **Ideas seem to float around** in a local psychosphere and are picked up by various open minds. Listen and you will also see or hear what you have recently been thinking or talking about from someone you don't know.
- Be careful about being too open to New Age promises.
- Telepathy that occurs in the same space probably has a different mechanism than telepathy at a distance. **Local telepathy** should have a different name since the *tele* in *tele*pathy means at a distance. Each of us has a bioenergetic field that contains information. I think it is possible to intuitively read information in that field.
- **Being out in nature**, away from the stimulations of homes, towns, and cities probably increases our capacity to pick up information from auras.
- You may receive an **answer to a question** without having to ask.
- Our environment, and those people in it, can **mirror our minds** perhaps because each mind operates within the same mental atmosphere, the psychosphere.

- Be alert in times of **need**. What you are seeking may be somewhere in the vicinity.
- Try to find value in the restrictions imposed on you by the context in which you are working.
- The **still, small voice** that comes to you, especially when immersed in nature, can help you prepare for the future. Those soft voices may be offering interesting possibilities. It seems you have to say yes!
- When the **need** arises, a solution may be on the horizon. Use your intuition, seize the opportunity! Various inputs to intuition can open the gates of synchronicity as we learn to use them through trial-and-error testing. Keep believing in the value of your intuitive messages.
- High emotion (**anger**) and life stressors (going out on my own) increase the likelihood of meaningful coincidences.
- Coincidences can be **remarkably positive and remarkably awful**. Either way, trying to comprehend their possible meaning becomes a challenge for each of us. While it is up to the person experiencing the synchronicity to interpret it, sometimes an external perspective can start the interpretation. If you have an idea about the possible meaning of a dramatic coincidence involving someone you know, at least offer it to get the person thinking about it again.
- Amazingly unlikely synchronicities do not necessarily lead to any outcome. **They just are.** They can illustrate the strange interconnections we have with others.
- To keep swinging from metaphorical **vine to vine** requires believing the next vine will appear close enough for you to grasp. Keep swinging, if that is your style.
- The **timing** of some coincidence sequences strengthens the confirmation of a decision. And they are often entertaining.
- Where you **focus your attention** increases the likelihood that you will see synchronicities bearing the content of what is passing through your own mind.
- Meaningful coincidences can be pleasurable as well as illuminate the invisible currents that connect and unify us. It's more evidence for the **internet of the mind** in the psychosphere.

- Does **telepathy** exist? The scientific data are pretty strong. My model requires two fundamental assumptions: (1) the existence of the psychosphere, and (2) each of us has a Higher Self floating around in the psychosphere.
- Current scientific researchers will continue to explore the mysteries of our expanding universe and the immense curiosities living in the depths of our oceans. A third **mystery is the human mind,** which deserves far more attention than it is getting. How, for example, do mind and brain connect with each other? The range of coincidences described in this book point toward innate human capacities worthy of disciplined study.
- **Birds** (and many other animals) are more like people than we rational thinkers are taught. Or perhaps we are more like animals than we like to believe.
- **Keep moving!** The more intersections you have with other beings and with things, the more likely meaningful coincidences will take place. Intersections are the fundamental elements of synchronicity. You can travel all over the world when what you are seeking is **right in front of you** at home.
- Manifestation is another name for producing **mind movies** of the desired future. In producing them, recognize your limitations as well as your abilities in 3D reality. Asking for more than you can handle or more than is possible from your environment will lead to disappointment.
- The primary way to find **parallels between people** is through dialogue.
- Timing may not be everything, but it sure helps. **Immerse yourself in the Now** and watch what sometimes happens. Try this play with the word *nowhere*. The word contains *now here*. You can be immersed in the infinity of Now and be both nowhere and right here now.
- Even naming the mystery "**The Name**" is a form of naming. Names cannot capture the vastness. Currently many people use *Universe*.

- Let **nature** open your mind.
- **Serendipity** is finding something you are not looking for, but when you see it, you recognize its value.
- The deeper you get into **living coincidence flow**, the more what you seek will probably come to you. Those voices in your head can be very helpful sometimes, especially when you know you need to listen.
- A coincidence involving a coincidence is a **meta-coincidence**. This coincidence category often makes minds swim in amazement. Coincidences can not only be suggestions, they **can be warnings** about an impending decision.
- Embrace the mirrors of your mind that coincidences can often be.
- **Dance can be like a gas station** where you can fill up on energy from others who have extra energy to express and exchange. Your energy may also feed them.
- Experienced dancers know that dance floor energy exists. Listen to **athletes describe how they feed off the energy of the crowd**. They know it is real. Open yourself up to the possibility.
- Try mastering your bioenergy field. It's important to **strengthen your energetic boundaries** to prevent others from creating negativity in your personal energy field. Meditating on your energetic boundaries can begin to help.
- Psychotherapists need to study the **energetic fit** between themselves and their patients. When they come home to their partners with low energy, they may have actually given all of it in the office. I think we will need to learn how to more efficiently conserve our energy outputs.
- Human minds are connected to our environment, not only to other people and animals and plants, but also to the machines we use. Many people have observed that **video and audio teleconferencing connections sometime become erratic** when intense emotions are sent through the internet. Sometimes it's random, sometimes direct cause and effect. The existence of fields of energy in and around us has been recognized by philosophical

systems around the world. Modern day energy workers seem to be working with the same energy fields. But none of these systems emphasize the existence of energy between people. Interpersonal energy deserves more direct discussion and research.

- **How need manifests the sought response** can be understood through the metaphor of the internet. You put in your request for needed information and a series of algorithms finds matches. The specificity of your request helps sharpen the results. I propose that parallel processes take place between your energized, emotionally charged thoughts and the "glove" wanting to cover your hand. Their specific energy-information signatures complement each other and draw them to you through the psychosphere, through this sparkling mental internet. We need further study about the conditions that increase these connections. Gratitude, need, and openheartedness seem to be necessary. Petition prayer. Being in the flow of evolving yourself and humanity seems to also increase the likelihood.

- **Jealousy**, competitiveness, and undercutting are unfortunately part of the behavior of humans in groups. Even if your team is unified in its goal directedness, be alert to those who might wish to undercut you. Serial coincidences like this can let you know.

- The heart generates emotional information that can be registered by others nearby.

- Taking chances requires being alert in the moment to avoid disaster.

- Fools rush in where angels fear to tread. Maybe because the angels know better. **Look before you leap**. These are time-tested aphorisms worth keeping in mind.

- Be grateful when you **survive near-death events** and continue to carry out what you have discovered to be your purpose in life. You will have to take a chance on chance, but not too chancy. The motorcycle race is an example of a foolish chance to take. Try to remember to weigh the cost and weigh the benefit.

Acknowledgments

IN MEDICAL SCHOOL, I imagined my moving body to be a pen writing my story on the canvas of life. Many people and places have provided colorful inks. Chief among them are my parents Karl and Anne Beitman, my brother Allen, and our many relatives in Wilmington, Delaware, and New York City, all of whom connected me through the generations. Paula Levine gave life to my sons Aaron and Karlen, who together provided a new foundation from which to continue this coincidence-filled life. My daughter-in-law Liza Roberts, grandchildren Zoe, Max, and Rose carry on by carrying on.

Places matter as do the people in them. Moreland Elementary School in Shaker Heights, Ohio; Edgemoor Elementary School and Mount Pleasant High School in Wilmington, Delaware; Swarthmore College; Yale Medical School; Mt. Zion Hospital and the U.S. Public Health Hospital and Haight-Ashbury in San Francisco; Stanford; University of Washington; Columbia, Missouri, and the University of Missouri; and now Charlottesville, Virginia.

The people who loved me.

Bob Warner, my best friend from high school; Coach John Michaelwicz who taught me how to drag bunt; English teacher Mr. Schomborg who showed me how to begin to feel; Hap Peelle, my brother in college baseball and football; and Randy Weingarten, a psychiatric colleague and loving friend from our Stanford residency.

At Sacred Planet Books, how very fortunate I am to be developing a friendship with Richard Grossinger. He knows so much and I've come to hear his speaking as a form of prose singing. Through him I've connected with the multitalented and wise Ruslana Remennikova.

And, at last, after journeying through many places, I have found an accepting and loving community in Charlottesville. Peter Richardson, John D'earth, Amalia Harte, Barbara Groves, Josh Silver, and the people of the Charlottesville dance co-op. Most importantly, Patrick Huyghe, the excellent editor of my three coincidence books, such a good guy!

Bibliography

Bass, Christopher, and Clyde Wade. "Chest Pain with Normal Coronary Arteries: A Comparative Study of Psychiatric and Social Morbidity." *Psychological Medicine* 14, no. 1 (1984): 51–61.

Beitman, B. *Connecting with Coincidence: The New Science for Using Synchronicity and Serendipity in Your Life.* Deerfield Beach, FL: Health Communications, 2016.

Beitman, B. *Meaningful Coincidences: How and Why Synchronicity and Serendipity Happen.* Rochester, VT: Park Street Press, 2022.

Beitman, Bernard, Niels C. Beck, William E. Deuser, Cameron S. Carter, J. R. Davidson, and Richard J. Maddock. "Patient Stage of Change Predicts Outcome in a Panic Disorder Medication Trial." *Anxiety* 1, no. 2 (1994): 64–69.

Crowley, Aleister. *The Book of Lies.* London: Wieland, 1913.

de Peyer, Janine. "Uncanny Communication and the Porous Mind." *Psychoanalytic Dialogues* 26, no. 2 (2016): 156–74.

Garfield, E., and H. Zuckerman. "Multiple Independent Discovery and Creativity in Science." In *Essays of an Information Scientist.* Vol. 4, *1979–1980.* Wilmington, DE: Institute for Scientific Information (ISI), 1980.

Jung, Carl Gustav. Foreword to *The I Ching or Book of Changes,* trans. Richard Wilhelm and Cary F. Baynes. London: Routledge, 1968.

Jung, C. G. "Synchronicity: An Acausal Connecting Principle." In *The Collected Works of C. G. Jung.* Vol. 8, *The Structure and Dynamics of the Psyche.* 2nd ed. Edited by H. Read et al., 417–519. London: Routledge & Kegan Paul, 1969. (Original work published 1952.)

Mackey, Chris. *The Positive Psychology of Synchronicity.* London: Watkins, 2019.

Main, Roderick. *Breaking the Spell of Disenchantment: Mystery, Meaning, and Metaphysics in the Work of C. G. Jung.* Asheville, NC: Chiron Publications, 2022.

Pahnke, Walter N. "Drugs and Mysticism." *International Journal of Parapsychology* 8, no. 2 (Spring 1966): 295–313.